Government to Government

Models of Cooperation Between States and Tribes

By
Susan Johnson
Jeanne Kaufmann
National Conference of State Legislatures

John Dossett
Sarah Hicks
National Congress of American Indians

NATIONAL CONFERENCE
of STATE LEGISLATURES
The Forum for America's Ideas

William T. Pound, Executive Director

1560 Broadway, Suite 700
Denver, Colorado 80202
(303) 830-2200

444 North Capitol Street, N.W.
Washington, D.C. 20001
(202) 624-5400

NATIONAL CONGRESS
OF AMERICAN INDIANS

Jacqueline Johnson, Executive Director

1301 Connecticut Ave., N.W.
Suite 200
Washington, D.C. 20036
(202) 466-7767

May 2002

The National Conference of State Legislatures is the bipartisan organization that serves the legislators and staffs of the states, commonwealths and territories.

NCSL provides research, technical assistance and opportunities for policymakers to exchange ideas on the most pressing state issues and is an effective and respected advocate for the interests of the states in the American federal system.

NCSL has three objectives:

- To improve the quality and effectiveness of state legislatures.
- To promote policy innovation and communication among state legislatures.
- To ensure state legislatures a strong, cohesive voice in the federal system.

The Conference operates from offices in Denver, Colorado, and Washington, D.C.

The National Congress of American Indians (NCAI) was founded in 1944 in response to termination and assimilation policies that the United States forced upon tribal governments in contradiction of their treaty rights and status as sovereigns. NCAI stressed the need for unity and cooperation among native governments for the protection of their treaty and sovereign rights. Since 1944, the National Congress of American Indians has been working to inform the public and Congress on the governmental rights of American Indians and Alaska Natives.

Now as in the past, NCAI serves to:

- Secure to ourselves and our descendants the rights and benefits to which we are entitled,
- Enlighten the public toward the better understanding of the Indian people,
- Preserve rights under Indian treaties or agreements with the United States, and
- Promote the common welfare of the American Indians and Alaska Natives.

On the cover: A quilt by Dallas, Texas, artist Myrna Johnson, entitled *Learning from the Past and Other Cultures*, uses traditional western patterns in bright contemporary colors inspired by Native American art.

Printed on recycled paper

©2002 by the National Conference of State Legislatures. All rights reserved.
ISBN 1-58024-231-6

Contents

About the Authors iv

Preface and Acknowledgments v

Executive Summary ix

1. Introduction: The Relationship Between Tribes and States 1
   Smart for States, Smart for Tribes 3
   The Devolution Factor 5

2. Guiding Principles in State-Tribal Relations 6
   A Commitment to Cooperation 7
   Mutual Understanding and Respect 7
   Regular and Early Communication 9
   Process and Accountability for Addressing Issues 10
   Institutionalization of Relationships 10

3. Legislative and Tribal Roles and Responsibilities 12
   The State Legislative Role 12
   Tribal Government Role 14

4. Models for Cooperation 16
   Section 1. State Legislative Committees 17
   Section 2. State Commissions and Offices 24
   Section 3. State-Tribal Government-to-Government
      Agreements and Protocols 32
   Section 4. Tribal Delegates in State Legislatures 41
   Section 5. Intertribal Organizations 45
   Section 6. Dedicated Indian Events at the Legislatures 48
   Section 7. Individual Legislator Efforts 52
   Section 8. State Recognition of Native Cultures
      and Governments 56
   Section 9. Training for Legislators and Tribal Leaders
      on Respective Government Processes 59
   Section 10. Other Potential Legislative Mechanisms 62

5. Conclusion 64

Appendix 65

References 85

ABOUT THE AUTHORS

This book was produced jointly by the National Conference of State Legislatures (NCSL) and the National Congress of American Indians (NCAI).

At NCSL, Susan Johnson was the project manager and Jeanne Kaufmann was a policy associate for the state-tribal relations project.

At NCAI, John Dossett and Sarah Hicks are the project managers and Andrea Arnold served as the project assistant for the state-tribal relations project.

PREFACE AND ACKNOWLEDGMENTS

This is the second publication of the National Conference of State Legislatures (NCSL)/National Congress of American Indians (NCAI) Project on Tribal-State Relations, a joint effort to promote intergovernmental cooperation between states and tribes by researching, assessing and disseminating information about how devolution of federal programs to state, tribal and local governments will affect Indian tribes and the state-tribal relationship.

The first publication, *Government to Government: Understanding State and Tribal Governments*, provides basic information to help promote understanding of tribal and state governments and the increasing need for cooperation between states and tribes. (Contact either organization if you would like to obtain a copy of this publication.)

This book is intended to more comprehensively examine existing models of state-tribal cooperation on a broad range of issues. Literally thousands of state and tribal laws, agreements and institutions help to facilitate tribal-state relations across the country; this book does not attempt to catalogue all of them. State and tribal leaders have generally expressed a view that, because of the unique relationships and history in each state, it is not helpful to try to directly emulate the experiences of other states. Instead, in recognition that the process of relationship building is as important as the product, this book highlights some of the broad strategies and institutions that tribes and states have used to build communication and respect between their governments. In addition, some key issue areas of tribal-state relations are highlighted in an attempt to develop a general understanding of how state and tribal governments in various states have been able to find common ground on these issues.

Much of the data in this volume were collected during project activities. NCSL and NCAI held two joint meetings of tribal leaders and state legislators—in Washington in late 2000 and in Wisconsin in early 2001. At those events, all state legislators and tribal leaders in those states were invited to discuss relevant issues and potential solutions and were provided opportunities to get to know each other. In June 2000, NCAI hosted its midyear meeting in Juneau, Alaska; tribal-state relations was the theme of the meeting. Similarly, at the NCSL annual meeting in Chicago in July 2000, a session focussed on state-tribal relations. NCSL and NCAI staff also have been involved in numerous other meetings—hosted by legislative committees, intertribal groups and others—where data were collected. Finally, an advisory council to this project has met several times and provided ideas and editorial comments on drafts of this document. We would like to thank the following advisory council members.

Chairman W. Ron Allen
Jamestown S'Klallam Tribe
Advisory Council Co-Chair

Senate Majority Leader Lana Oleen
Kansas
Advisory Council Co-chair

Senator Dennis Bercier
North Dakota

David Lovell, Senior Analyst
Wisconsin Legislative Council Staff

Chairman Robert Chicks
Stockbridge-Munsee Band
of Mohican Indians

John McCoy, Executive Director
Intergovernmental Relations
Tulalip Tribes

Senator Kelly Haney
Oklahoma

Senator Tim Sheldon
Washington

LaDonna Harris, President
Americans for Indian Opportunity

Preface and Acknowledgments

Thanks also to Chairperson Pearl Baller, Quinault Nation; Chairperson Colleen Cawston, Confederated Tribes of the Colville Reservation; Chairman Brian Cladoosby, Swinomish Tribe; Joe Day, Executive Director, Minnesota Indian Affairs Council; The Great Lakes Inter-Tribal Council; Cyndi Holmes, Self Governance Director, Jamestown S'Klallam Tribe; Joyce Kiel, Senior Staff Attorney, Wisconsin Legislative Council; John Lewis, Executive Director, Inter-Tribal Council of Arizona; Representative Terry M. Musser, Wisconsin; Alan Parker, Evergreen State College; Karen Quigley, Executive Director, Oregon Legislative Commission on Indian Affairs; and Barbara Warner, Executive Director, Oklahoma Indian Affairs Commission.

NCSL publications staff members Leann Stelzer and Scott Liddell edited and formatted the document.

Finally, special thanks go to the W.K. Kellogg Foundation, for realizing the importance of and providing funding for this effort.

Executive Summary

There are many remarkably successful new developments in state-tribal relations to consider. As Indian tribes build capacity and more frequently exercise their powers of self-government, tribal and state governments are increasingly finding areas of mutual interest and discovering ways to set aside jurisdictional rivalry in favor of cooperative government-to-government interactions. Tribes and states have been creating entirely new structures for communication and collaboration, solutions and agreements have been created for the ever-changing range of issues, and older tribal-state institutions have been strengthened and revived.

At the same time, the development of positive intergovernmental relationships between states and tribes has been uneven. In one state there may be development of improved communications and a building sense of trust between state and tribal officials, while in a neighboring state the parties will rarely speak to each other. Within the same state, there may be a great deal of cooperation on one issue but very little on another. Finally, it is common to find a creative and mutually beneficial solution for a particular policy issue in one state, while many other states and tribes continue to struggle—without resolution—with essentially the same issue.

The antagonistic history of state-tribal jurisdictional battles, the lack of understanding about navigating respective government bureaucracies, and a lack of widespread dialogue about the potential benefits of governmental cooperation are tensions that consistently underlie attempts at establishing state-tribal relations. Specifically, state-tribal relationships may be influenced by state-perceived negatives, such as the loss of jurisdictional control, tax base and land. Tribes also may approach the relationship with trepidation, history and the tribal-federal relationship often hamper tribal motivation to work with state government.

Sometimes, rather than actively opposing each other's positions on issues, states and tribes may simply avoid one another, choosing instead to ignore their neighboring government and any opportunity to cooperatively address mutual interests. These dynamics often may lead states and tribes that are attempting to develop working relations to feel as through they are sailing uncharted territory.

By recognizing some guiding principles in effective state-tribal relations and highlighting examples of successful cooperative government, this book is intended to assist tribes and states as they explore new avenues in their continuing efforts to improve governmental service for the citizens of both tribes and states.

1. Introduction: The Relationship Between Tribes and States

Numerous barriers exist to effective state-tribal relations. Outdated perceptions of American Indian tribes continue to prevail in non-Indian communities, and state officials may not understand that tribes are functioning governments. Sometimes, when state officials do recognize tribes as governments, they assume that tribal governments do not have the capacity or jurisdiction to relate to state government on a government-to-government basis. Tribes, on the other hand, may be hesitant to form working relationships with state governments because of tribes' constitutional and direct relationship with the federal government. Tribes have feared that interacting and building relationships with state governments would mitigate or diminish the federal trust responsibility and federal government-to-tribal government relationship.

As any government at any level in the United States finds today, relationships between political units can be challenging and complex. Against the intricately woven backdrop of federal, tribal, state and local laws and regulations, multiple interconnections and interdependence complicate these dynamic and vital relationships. But as Jemez Pueblo Governor Raymond Gachupin told New Mexico legislators, "We are your neighbors. We are your friends ... We are your constituents. And, most importantly, we are your fellow New Mexicans."

There are many good reasons to strive for cooperation. Any two or more neighboring governments, as a practical matter, share many aspects of their respective economic and social systems and are connected through political and legal relationships. These connections create an inevitable interdependence. Wisconsin Representative John Ainsworth, whose district neighbors are the Stockbridge-Munsee and the Menominee reservations, recognizes the tribal, state and local governments "sink or swim together." At the 2000 Indian Day at the New Mexico Legislature, Sara Misquez, president of the Mescalero Apache Tribe, suggested state lawmakers " ... set aside old stereotypes and begin a new chapter in our governmental relations. Our futures, whether we realize it or not, are most assuredly intertwined."

Mutual interests are clear. Both states and tribes want to use resources effectively and efficiently, provide comprehensive services and a safe environment for citizens, protect natural environments, and sustain healthy economies. The ultimate—even if not specific—governmental goals are the same.

Effective state-tribal government relations can reduce the unintended consequences of state legislative and administrative actions on tribal governments and, likewise, the consequences of tribal actions on surrounding areas. Even where the parties truly desire to cooperate, it is much more expensive and difficult to change a decision after it has been made. Increased general state-tribal dialogue can sensitize governments to the interests of each party and provide a forum for discussion about the potential effects of specific governmental actions on neighboring governments before decisions are made.

Overall, it seems that successful intergovernmental relationships are forged when individuals on both sides have invested leadership and good will in reaching out to find solutions. Says Senator Lana Oleen, Kansas Senate majority leader, "I, for one, do believe that cooperation, not confrontation, is the way not only to resolve difference, but also to heighten awareness of our respective responsibilities as elected leaders."

Introduction: The Relationship Between States and Tribes

Smart for States, Smart for Tribes

State-tribal relationships can be mutually beneficial, helping neighboring governments generally to do their jobs more effectively and also yielding many specific benefits. Effective state-tribal relationships, for example, help states serve their tribal citizens. All tribal members also are citizens of the state in which they reside, and all tribal lands lie within state legislative districts. As such, tribal members are eligible for state services and programs, just as any other state citizens. The difficulty for states in serving these particular citizens, however, often lies in cultural differences or the remoteness of populations. By working together, state and tribal governments can find the best way to provide services to these unique populations without wasting valuable resources on ineffective programs.

Building state-tribal relationships can create an opportunity for tribal governments to contract for the administration of some state programs on Indian lands. While relieving the state of its obligation to provide services to a particular group of people that frequently may be "hard-to-serve" because they reside on-reservation in a remote, rural area, tribally administered programs also can benefit both the state and tribes by meeting the specific needs of tribal citizens and using their particular cultural philosophies in the design of their programs, whether for managing natural resources, sustaining a healthy environment, or providing assistance to tribal members in a culturally appropriate manner and environment. Additionally, exercising tribal self-determination by interacting with state governments on the basis of tribal governmental status can serve to reinforce tribal sovereignty, rather than to diminish it, as some tribal leaders fear.

Positive tribal-state relations also can reduce legal problems. Both tribes and states have erred in first seeking a conclusive legal opinion about who has jurisdiction over a particular matter. Given the unclear state of federal Indian law, this formula can produce a significant amount of time-consuming, expensive litigation that may produce unpredictable and undesirable results for all parties.

National Conference of State Legislatures / National Congress of American Indians

The citizens who live in and around Indian reservations have a right to expect that the state and tribal governments first will seek to cooperate wherever possible to provide the best possible government services. By seeking cooperation, state and tribal governments also can avoid duplicating services unnecessarily.

As the Alaska Commission on Rural Governance and Empowerment noted, "Collaborative arrangements among municipal, tribal, regional, state and federal governments, institutions and agencies provide the means for strengthened local self-governance. Increased participation in decision making, more efficient service provision, and more effective management of environmental, land, and fish and game resources are results of cooperative efforts."

Economic development often can be enhanced by effective tribal-state partnerships. Economic development helps infuse resources into the tribal economy, allowing for greater development of human capital, providing jobs on reservations, and assisting tribes to become self-sufficient. State governments also benefit from tribal economic development, both directly (taxation and gaming compact payments) and indirectly (increased tribal revenue and spending, purchase of goods and services from surrounding, off-reservation businesses). Studies consistently show that tribal economic growth contributes significantly to surrounding communities.

Open communication about economic conditions, sectors, markets and opportunities potentially can increase economic benefits and decrease economic risks for both governments. States also may realize the importance of federal money that goes to tribes and, ultimately, to the shared economy. Finally, state governments benefit from the jobs that tribes create; many non-Indian people work for businesses owned by tribal governments. As W. Ron Allen, chairman of the Jamestown S'Klallam Tribe has recognized, "As the Indian communities become healthy, so does the state. Automatically."

The Devolution Factor

The transfer of federal resources and responsibilities to state, local or tribal governments—often through federal block grants or other funding mechanisms—is commonly referred to as devolution. This shift of authority away from the federal government is intended to make governments more responsive to local needs. In recent years, a variety of governmental functions have been devolved from the federal government to states and, to differing degrees, to tribal governments. This trend is likely to continue across a broad range of federal programs.

The devolution of federal authorities and resources to state, tribal and local governments has increased the opportunity for and the benefits of enhanced state-tribal relations. More than ever, states and tribes find themselves with parallel or overlapping responsibilities and many incentives for cooperation. According to Stephen Cornell, the director of the Udall Center for Studies in Public Policy at the University of Arizona, and Jonathan Taylor of the Udall Center and the Harvard Project on American Indian Economic Development:

> [T]ribes and states are in relationships that are much more complex and uncertain that ever before. . . . The evidence is compelling that where tribes have taken advantage of the federal self-determination policy to gain control of their own resources and of economic and other activity within their borders, and have backed up that control with good governance, they have invigorated their economies and produced positive economic spillovers to states.

Devolution is bringing policymaking to the local level, which provides opportunities for communities to have more influence over policies that will effect them. For state, tribal and local policymaking to be successful, however, neighboring governments will want to consider collaborating and, at least, coordinating the making of policy and administration of programs.

2. Guiding Principles in State-Tribal Relations

Most of the time and energy dedicated to tribal-state relations is spent on specific issues, such as fishing rights or health care reimbursement formulas. However, underlying factors contribute greatly to success on the specific issues and relationships in general. Of all the state-tribal relationships, institutions and agreements in various states, one particular mechanism does not appear to be inherently better than another. Instead, general principles and functions have been shown to lead to better working relationships. For example, why does a particular legislative "Committee on Indian Affairs" get good results? Perhaps because it provides a well-accepted forum for both legislators and tribal leaders to work out issues, and it facilitates the sharing of information on a regular basis. Is a "Committee on Indian Affairs" the only mechanism available to do this? Actually, many state commissions and inter-tribal councils serve a similar function. It is the function that matters, not the specific mechanism that might be used to achieve that function. The principles that provide the basis for these functions are cooperation, understanding, communication, process and institutionalization. State legislators and tribal leaders can use these principles in their work together, as well as in their oversight of the administrative branches of their governments.

> **Principles That Guide Good Working Relationships**
> - Cooperation
> - Understanding and Respect
> - Communication
> - Process
> - Institutionalization

Guiding Principles in State-Tribal Relations

A Commitment to Cooperation

Public attention often is focused on the conflicts found in the state-tribal relationship, and certainly there have been many conflicts in areas such as land claims, water rights, hunting and fishing, taxation and gaming. Perhaps because of these high-profile conflicts, a common view of state-tribal relations is that they consist solely of competition for control. This view is not so much wrong as it is incomplete.

The great bulk of the interactions between Indian tribes and states are not at all controversial. The reality is that, at the local level in and around tribal lands, tribes, states and local governments daily cooperate and share responsibilities for government services on a broad range of issues. Tribes have jurisdiction over some matters, states have jurisdiction over others, and in many areas jurisdiction is shared or undetermined.

State and tribal leaders may understand, in theory, why cooperation makes sense. One benefit could be the resources saved by avoiding litigation and duplication of services. For relations to be successful, however, all involved need to make a genuine commitment to relationship building and cooperation.

"Both sides must be willing to go more than halfway," says Senator Lana Oleen, majority leader for the Kansas Senate. "You must be willing to reach out if you want to come to an agreement. Reaching an agreement is worth the extra effort because the solution will last much longer and we can tailor the agreement to meet our specific needs."

Mutual Understanding and Respect

Although it may seem obvious that any relationship must be based on mutual understanding and respect, this is an especially distinct concern in tribal-state relations. Many individual legislators and other state government officials often have not dealt with tribal issues enough to sufficiently understand the governmental status of Indian tribes. Public education does not teach that tribes are governments, and many adults—including state legislators—perceive tribes and tribal members as minorities or special interest groups.

Tribal understanding and respect of state governments also are needed. Tribal leaders often have a great deal of mistrust about state government based on historical dealings with the state. Building trust through a course of forthright relationships will be the only way to repair that trust. In addition to understanding that statehood and state sovereignty are important cultural factors for many state officials, some tribal leaders may not be well informed about how state government functions. Multi-layered state bureaucracy can make "navigating the state system almost impossible," says Steve Gobin, governmental affairs liaison for the Tulalip Tribes. Successful state-tribal relations must include an education mechanism to help to establish this mutual understanding, acceptance and credibility both in terms of general understanding of the intergovernmental dynamic and understanding of the parties' concerns about specific issues.

W. Ron Allen, chairman of the Jamestown S'Klallam Tribe, put it this way: "It is very difficult to accomplish anything with the state if every time you meet with someone you have to justify who you are and why you have a right to be involved. Tribes have treaties with the federal government and we are recognized in the U.S. Constitution, but we often have to teach that to every state official we meet. How are we supposed to get into the details of an issue on fisheries or taxes, if we can't get past the ABCs?"

In speaking to a group of state legislators and staff, Stephen Pevar, senior staff counsel for the American Civil Liberties Union, recognized that understanding and respect goes both ways: "Indian tribes should spend time in their state legislatures, getting to know their legislators and to understand how the policymaking process works. Likewise, legislators should gain a better understanding of their neighboring tribes, getting to know the tribal leadership and community. Legislators should listen to what tribes have to say, even if it is very different—particularly if it is very different—from the way that legislators traditionally think about and look at things."

The Alaska Commission on Rural Governance and Empowerment echoed, "Native cultures bring a valuable non-Western viewpoint and strength to society and government. Many of the environmental, social and political problems facing our society have not been solved through traditional Western solutions. Native perspectives offer alternative and possibly more effective ways to handle these issues."

Regular and Early Communication

Too often, tribes and states do not communicate regularly. Frequently, contacts are reactive and are made only after a conflict occurs. This is not a healthy dynamic for any relationship. Many conflicts are based on a simple misunderstanding or oversight. By the time a conflict boils over, however, the two sides may be locked into their positions, and the situation becomes more difficult to resolve. In addition, once an issue or crisis has escalated, it is time-consuming to determine who to talk to and difficult to establish relationships and build the necessary trust to work out solutions. It is better if relationships can be established before an issue arises.

The most effective state-tribal relationships include mechanisms that create and encourage ongoing communication between appropriate parties for any particular issue so that issues can be addressed in a timely manner. As Indian law professor and tribal judge, Frank Pommersheim noted in his 1995 book, *Braid of Feathers*, "One of the principal problems of tribal-state relations is the absence of forums—both formal and informal—in which Indians and non-Indians and tribal and state officials come together to discuss important issues. Given this lack, the resulting gulf in communication is all too easily filled with pernicious gossip and relentless stereotypes." Washington Representative Val Ogden agrees. "We need to know how bills will affect Indian tribes. We need a process to communicate on an ongoing basis, not just in a crisis."

Process and Accountability for Addressing Issues

The resolution of issues between tribes and states often is hindered by a lack of attention and follow-through. Processes that address these needs include 1) regular meetings, activities and communication between tribal governments and the branches and agencies of the state and other governments as appropriate; 2) a regular review and assessment of policies on issues related to tribal-state relations and provision of services; and 3) the provision of recommendations for improvements. It is also important to ensure that the issues those involved deem important are addressed and that issues are not over-generalized or linked to other, disparate issues. Sometimes, both states and tribes express a desire to include a broad sweep of issues within a single discussion or negotiation. As appealing as it might be to attempt to resolve a large number of issues at once, this more often than not can lead to an impasse on all issues. State officials might consider that wide differences among tribes in their priorities, cultures and resources prevent generic solutions. Likewise, tribal leaders may fail to understand state bureaucracy and its inherent limitations. Individual legislators, for instance, are part of a larger body and may not be able to immediately resolve an issue, and state agency officials have authority in only one general area.

Successful state-tribal relationships include mechanisms to address these issues. In particular, for a mechanism to effectively meet these needs, adequate staff and resources must be committed by all. Coordination among the various state and tribal branches, agencies and entities also is important to avoid duplication and intraparty conflict. For instance, if an office of Indian affairs is housed in the governor's office, the legislature may not be adequately included and tribes may find it necessary to duplicate their efforts in the legislature.

Institutionalization of Relationships

Finally, state-tribal relationships are influenced by mechanisms that institutionalize or preserve the relationship. Institutionalization—the creation of a permanent relationship method—provides certainty for both governments regarding the forum for intergovernmental relations and the process through which issues are addressed. Institutionalization also affects the ability of the intergovernmental relationship to withstand changes in tribal and state leadership and in political parties. This frequent and often large turnover in legislative and tribal council membership in general "… discourages a grasp of the larger (intergovernmental) issues," according to Washington Senator Tim Sheldon. Effective relationship mechanisms must be institutionalized to preserve the structure and gains of the relationship and to establish a base for further intergovernmental work.

Government-to-Government Relationships

Legislators and tribal leaders have asked for a practical definition of a government-to-government relationship. How can a tribe or numerous tribes have an intergovernmental relationship with a state legislature, when there is constant turnover and substantial diversity within both groups?

A successful government-to-government relationship between a legislature and one or more tribes involves several areas of understanding and cooperation.

- There is a mutual—and ongoing—understanding between both parties that each is an independent government that works for respective constituencies. As such, the state-tribal relationship is fundamentally an intergovernmental relationship.

- Both states and tribes understand that the relationship is unique, not only because all tribal citizens are state citizens and legislative constituents, but also because of the nature of the tribal-federal relationship.

- One or more mechanisms exist that facilitate the intergovernmental relationship between the state legislature and tribal leaders. Such mechanisms allow the states and tribes to maintain their respective governmental roles and responsibilities and to collaborate when appropriate.

- Both sides try to reach agreement on common issues, but recognize that there will always be some areas of conflict. These areas of conflict should not be allowed to influence the entire intergovernmental relationship.

3. Legislative and Tribal Roles and Responsibilities

The State Legislative Role

Legislatures and individual legislators can fulfill their roles in state-tribal relations in many ways. The most obvious is to address issues of shared governance in state policy through informed legislation. Under state constitutions, legislatures have general lawmaking powers. Although they may agree that governors will make policy decisions in specific areas, legislatures, rather than executive branch agencies, generally make the initial political decisions that balance competing interests. Every year, legislatures consider hundreds of bills that specifically affect American Indians, and many of these bills become law. These statutes address topics such as economic development, natural resources, health and human services, gaming, education, taxation and cultural issues. Legislatures also establish mechanisms for state-tribal relations such as those discussed in this book.

State legislatures do not operate in a vacuum. Legislative policy decisions are implemented—and often are proposed—by the executive branch, including the governor. Many governors have taken the lead in initiating a formal state-tribal relationship but gubernatorial efforts may not outlast the administration in which they were created. Likewise, many state agencies have taken innovative steps in relating to tribes without waiting for specific statutory authorization. However, legislative support—in the form of funding and statutory authority—will guarantee that such innovative steps will be more permanent and farther reaching. Successful agency programs—including state-tribal agreements and other services to tribal communities—can be codified into permanent requirements that outlast administration changes. Although many state-tribal relationships are acted out between state and tribal agency staff with regard to particular programs, the legislative role is crucial in regard to agency operations. Enacting enabling legislation, establishing specific program authority, controlling the makeup and operation of rulemaking entities, and overseeing rulemaking are typical functions within the legislative purview.

Many legislatures have passed legislation to encourage, require or ratify specific state-tribal agreements or to provide a framework for the state to enter into agreements with tribes—both in general and in specific issue areas. Montana (§18-11-101 to 18-11-112), Nebraska (§13-1501 to 13-1509), North Dakota (§54-40.2-01 to §54-40.2-09), and Wisconsin (§66.0301(2)), for instance, have similar comprehensive legislation that authorizes state agencies or political subdivisions to enter into agreements with tribes to perform virtually any government function. Many of these laws provide a framework for what should be included in agreements and establish processes for entering into, finalizing and revoking agreements. Oklahoma law (§1221) simply allows the governor and political subdivisions to enter into cooperative agreements "on issues of mutual interest," and directs that the agreements become effective upon approval by the legislature's Joint Committee on State-Tribal Relations. Many states have subject-specific agreement authorizations. Gaming, taxation, fish and wildlife, human services and other issues all are subjects of state laws that authorize agreements with Indian tribes.

Although both state agencies and governors have substantial roles in proposing state budgets, state legislatures appropriate all state spending, which has powerful implications both for a state's relationships with tribes and for tribal government functions. Expenditures from federal funding, fees, general state funds and other sources must be legislatively approved. The state legislature's budget or appropriations committees also set substantive policy through performance-based budgeting. This trend increases the potential for legislative involvement in agency priority setting.

Another legislative role in state-tribal relations involves constituent services. Tribal members are state citizens, so individual legislators are directly accountable to tribal members in their districts and have a responsibility to be informed about and be accessible to those constituencies. This includes understanding what it means to have a tribal government in one's district and the implications of these intergovernmental relationships. Such understanding also is helpful in responding to concerns of non-Indian constituents, who may not understand tribal governments. As discussed in more detail in chapter 4, there are many ways legislators can work with American Indian constituents and the unique tribal communities to which they belong.

Tribal Government Role

Tribal governments share with state governments the responsibility for building successful working relationships. Tribal government leaders have a responsibility to be informed about state legislatures and their decision-making processes. Tribes monitor legislative activities, provide input into legislative processes, and often take the initiative to make specific legislative proposals. Tribal councils also pass tribal laws that authorize cooperation with the state and with state programs.

Tribal governments also are responsible for building relationships with state elected officials. All Indian lands fall within established legislative districts. Legislators who represent districts that include tribal lands often have a smaller official to constituent ratio and, thus, an opportunity to develop closer constituent relationships and gain a greater sense of local conditions. Many tribal leaders find it helpful to take their state legislators on a tour of the reservation and the government services that the tribe provides. Such activities help state officials understand the tribe's goals and needs.

Tribal governments also participate in existing state-tribal forums, such as legislative committees and commissions. When tribal governments actively participate and take a role in bringing issues to the table, the utility and benefit of such forums to both governments are enhanced. Tribal governments also participate in consultation. For instance, tribes may consult with state government on issues of mutual concern in the state budget development process. Such consultation may help to prevent disputes and, in general, can lead to better relations. In order to make their positions known and contribute to the development of sound policy, tribes must attend consultation sessions, educate decision makers and provide constructive testimony.

Tribes can be involved in legislative processes either directly or indirectly. Tribal government officials, staff or tribal members may represent tribes in the state legislative process. Tribes also sometimes work collectively through an intertribal association. As an alternative, an attorney or lobbyist—who can assist in tracking state legislative processes and advocate for legislative proposals that benefit tribal governments—may represent tribes. Lobbyists may provide useful services in monitoring legislation, building relationships with legislators, and providing input into legislative processes, but tribal lobbyists may need to work to overcome a general perception that lobbyists represent "special interests," as opposed to tribal governments.

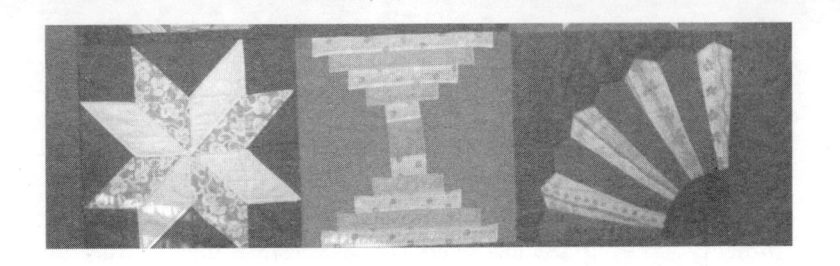

4. MODELS FOR COOPERATION

Recently, tribal and state governments have demonstrated a growing interest in creating institutions that facilitate improved tribal-state relations. A variety of mechanisms can contribute to improved intergovernmental relationships; these models have evolved differently in various states. Because of the diversity of state and tribal histories, resources and current circumstances, different models may best suit the needs of different states and tribes. In other words, although a variety of models exist, no one model works best in every situation. States and tribes that are interested in developing and maintaining intergovernmental relationships will want to consider the mechanisms as tools in a tool box, all of which may serve different functions in the relationship, none of which are mutually exclusive and most of which are mutually reinforcing.

> **Ten Mechanisms or Institutions that May Facilitate Improved Intergovernmental Relationships**
> - State Legislative Committees
> - State Commissions and Offices
> - State-Tribal Government-to-Government Agreements and Protocols
> - Tribal Delegates in State Legislatures
> - Intertribal Organizations
> - Dedicated Indian Events at the Legislatures
> - Individual Legislator Efforts
> - State Recognition of Native Cultures and Governments
> - Training for Legislators and Tribal Leaders on Respective Government Processes
> - Other Potential Legislative Mechanisms

Summarized below are 10 mechanisms or institutions—and some examples—that may serve to facilitate improved intergovernmental relationships.

Section 1. State Legislative Committees

Approximately 14 states have 17 different legislative committees to address Indian issues. Although many states have created Indian affairs committees in the past several years, some states have had these forums for decades. Wisconsin's Special Committee on State-Tribal Relations, for example, was established in 1955. A legislative committee—standing, interim or study—can act as a liaison between the legislature and tribal governments and can address issues of state-tribal relations in general. Legislative committees study specific issues and may propose, review or introduce legislation. A legislative committee on Indian affairs or state-tribal relations with authority to vote on legislation certainly could substantially affect the lawmaking process and exert political clout with agency directors and staff.

Whether such committees are effective depends first of all upon strong, proactive committee leadership, as well as on adequate staff support, member participation, and the powers and jurisdiction of the committee. Effective membership is representative of both the state population and the tribal population where there are tribal members on the committee, and that representation should survive state legislative and tribal leader turnover or administration changes. Some form of tribal participation also is crucial. It has proven counterproductive if the tribes are not involved in discussions about issues that affect them. "We never knew why they were gathering, it never came back to us," said Blackfeet Chair Earl Old Person of the now-defunct Montana Senate Committee on Indian Affairs (since replaced with the State-Tribal Relations Committee).

Although legislative committees are instruments of the state, some legislatures have found it beneficial to make the creation and operation of the committee a joint undertaking between the state and the tribes. This ensures that committee action is based on both mutual commitment and mutual needs, and parties feel free to discuss relevant issues. Some important points to consider when establishing such a committee:

- Indian issues cut across party lines, so it may be helpful to establish bipartisan leadership or alternating leadership between political parties.

- Flexibility in committee operation is important, so that formal procedures do not create barriers to full participation.

- Alternating meeting locations between the state capitol and sites on Indian lands will build a shared commitment to the functioning of the committee.

Wisconsin Special Committee on State-Tribal Relations

The Wisconsin Special Committee on State-Tribal Relations dates to 1955, when it was formed as the committee on Menominee Indians, the purpose of which was to address issues related to "the termination" of the Menominee Indian Tribe. Today, the committee—made up of 11 legislative members and nine tribal representatives—is " ... directed to study issues relating to American Indians and the American Indian tribes and bands in (the) state and develop specific recommendations and legislative proposals relating to these issues" (Wisc. Stats. 13.83(3)). It also serves an oversight function by reviewing selected executive branch actions regarding state-tribal relations and by facilitating communications between state and municipal agency officials and tribal officials. A technical advisory committee of representatives from seven state agencies assists the committee in its functions.

Although the committee has had a difficult time securing consistent attendance from both legislators and tribal members, it has had many successes during the last few decades. Some examples of areas in which the committee forged solutions include the creation of a county-tribal cooperative law enforcement program, establishment of full faith and credit in state courts for the actions of tribal courts and legislatures, protection of human burial sites, economic development on Indian reservations and Indian health issues. "It's amazing what can happen when people talk to each other," says Representative Terry Musser, the committee's current chair.

The committee provides for a strong tribal role. Tribal leaders help set the agenda by bringing issues to the attention of the committee. For instance, at the urging of gaiashkibos, chair of the Lac Courte Oreilles Band of Lake Superior Chippewa, the committee has been discussing the issue of tribal delegates to the Legislature (see section 4). Tribal members also participate in voting on committee recommendations. This process allows legislators to make better informed policy on these issues.

The committee does not address all state-tribal issues. For example, budgetary issues have been handled within the committees of jurisdiction, and gaming issues have largely been addressed through negotiations with the governor. The committee has been very active during the last few years. In March 2001, it co-hosted the *Wisconsin Leadership Conference on State-Tribal Relations*. The conference offered an opportunity for tribal and state leaders to hear what other states are doing to improve relationships with tribal governments and to discuss priorities and ideas for Wisconsin. Largely as a result of this conference and the ongoing involvement of the committee, several bills were introduced in the 2001-2002 session to deal with state-tribal relations. These include AJR 90, which urges the governor and state agencies to create consultation policies with tribal governments (see section 3); AJR 91, which would recognize the sovereign status of federally recognized tribes in Wisconsin; AB 771, which would create a tribal-state council; and AB 772, which would require "tribal impact statements" for bills that would affect tribal governments or American Indians (see section 10).

Wyoming Select Committee on State-Tribal Relations

The Wyoming Select Committee on State-Tribal Relations is an example of a new committee that is focused on establishing communication. The Legislature's Management Council created it in 2000 to "establish a process for better state/tribal relationships." The purpose of the committee, which consists of three senators and three representatives, is to act as a liaison between the Legislature and Indian tribes in the state. According to the chairman, Representative Harry Tipton, before the committee was established the tribes were presenting their points of view to the media. Since the formation of the committee, however, the tribes are coming to the legislators and the committee members to talk about issues. Ivan Posey, Chairman of the Eastern Shoshone Tribe, recognizes that tribes " ... have our own unique issues because of our relationship with the state. The key is to educate other legislators across the state and it is our responsibility to do so." Likewise, Representative Tipton believes that the tribes now understand the state process better and are making use of the committee contacts.

Senator Mark Harris, another committee member, is encouraged by its creation and believes the most important function of the committee is to develop a rapport between the Legislature and the tribes. "The ability to work together will allow us to learn to develop the ability to identify solvable issues, and give us solutions that will improve both the states and the tribes." Posey agrees, and hopes that the committee will remain active and functioning. The first meeting of the committee was held with the Joint Business Council of the Northern Arapaho and Eastern Shoshone tribes of the Wind River Reservation, which includes six elected members of each tribe. Although Representative Tipton does not anticipate much legislation, communication is the primary goal; both sides agree that the committee is a good first step in opening the lines of communication and acknowledging tribal issues.

California Assembly's Select Committee on Native American Repatriation

The California Assembly Select Committee on Native American Repatriation, formed in 1999, is an example of committee formed to discuss a discrete issue but that ultimately served as a forum to discuss broader issues. Ten Assembly members made up the committee, which was originally formed to determine the disposition of the brain of Ishi, the last member of the Yahi Indian Tribe of California. Chairman of the committee, Assemblyman Darrell Steinberg, stated that, "Select committees can really have value and this is an example where it has. The nice thing about this type of committee is that you can take one idea and, over the course of a year or so, make a difference because you can focus on that issue and it will receive more attention." Steinberg had never dealt with tribes or repatriation and was astonished at the magnitude of the issue. Ishi's brain subsequently was buried with the rest of his remains in northern California, but the committee continues to deal with other Native American issues.

Assemblyman Steinberg was approached by the Barona Band of Mission Indians, who invited him and other interested parties to southern California to discuss, on a larger scale, the issue of repatriation. The purpose of the subsequent hearing was to allow the tribes, museum officials and academicians to voice to state legislators their opinions and views on repatriation. Tribal Councilman Steve Banegas said that, "Once we heard about the select committee and met with Steinberg, we were able to present the idea of legislation and work together to pass it into law."

A bipartisan bill (Assembly Bill 978), which became law in October 2001, expedites compliance with the federal Native American Graves Protection and Repatriation Act of 1990 and ensures enforcement of the return of remains and objects. This state version of the federal act also creates the Repatriation Oversight Committee and includes penalties for noncompliance with the law.

Assemblyman Steinberg says the bill has "sensitized members of the Legislature to an issue few were aware of" and extends beyond committee members to academics and professionals as well as to the general public. David Baron, government affairs liaison for the Barona Band of Mission Indians, who also worked in the Assembly, was encouraged by support for the bill because there were "more co-authors on this bill than any I've ever seen." Baron also is encouraged by the people he has met in the Legislature and during the committee hearing on repatriation. "They [the tribes] have shown legislators that the tribes are interested in issues, and legislators now are more aware of tribal commitment and involvement."

New Mexico's Joint Committee on Compacts

A very different example of an issue-specific committee arose in New Mexico to deal with a serious controversy over Indian gaming. Indian gaming in New Mexico began in 1984 with high-stakes bingo games in the Acoma Pueblo's community gym. Since then, Indian gaming in New Mexico has grown substantially, but the road has not been smooth. The federal Indian Gaming Regulatory Act, passed in 1988, instructs states and tribes to enter into compacts for Indian gaming. The law does not define which branch of the "state" government is responsible for the negotiating and decision making on behalf of the state; all three branches of the New Mexico state government have been involved in the issue. Governor Gary Johnson signed several compacts with the tribes in 1995, but the New Mexico Supreme Court quickly struck down the compacts (*New Mexico ex rel. Clark vs. Johnson*, 1995), holding that the governor had performed a legislative function. The issue remained on court dockets and was under consideration in the Legislature during the next several years.

The years of confusion and controversy set the stage for the Legislature to create the permanent Joint Legislative Committee on Compacts in 1999 (N.M. Stat. 11-13A-1 to 11-13A-5). The committee is comprised of eight members from the House and eight members from the Senate, who represent an equal number of Democrats and Republicans. Leadership must consider appointing legislators who are Native American or who represent a district in which a "significant percentage" of voters are Native American.

The committee meets as needed to review proposed compacts or amendments after they have been negotiated by the governor with the tribes. Changes recommended by the committee are renegotiated with the tribes by the governor's office. Once the committee approves a compact, the Legislature as a whole then must approve it before the governor can execute it. The Legislature, however, can only approve or reject the proposed compact but cannot amend it.

The process appears to work. The committee agreed to 11 new identical compacts with 11 gaming tribes during the 2001 legislative session, and the compacts were approved by the entire Legislature on March 12, 2001. The new compacts, which lower the rate of revenue-sharing payments tribes would pay to the state, were signed by Governor Johnson and approved by the U.S. Department of Interior that same year.

After years of uncertainty and contention, the parties appeared to be generally committed to cooperation. "The compact was negotiated in good faith," said Representative James Taylor. "I think that was something that people felt was missing the last time." Richard Hughes, who represented the pueblos of Santa Ana and Santa Clara and was one of the tribes' lead negotiators in general, noted that, "The committee members worked hard, and the tribes tried to be responsive to all the concerns that were raised."

The series of committee meetings during two years brought together tribal leaders and legislators who otherwise might not interact. In this sense, the committee promoted interactions on a government-to-government basis that led to increased understanding among legislators and tribal leaders of each others' governments and interests. The process seemed to set a positive tone for future relations, according to Senator John Arthur Smith, who chaired the committee in 2000. Governor Johnson believes the compacts represent " ... the beginning of a new age in tribal-state relations in New Mexico ... (and the process proves) that the Tribes and the state can reach results on a government-to-government basis," according to the governor's correspondence to the Secretary of Interior after the compacts were approved by the Legislature.

Senator Smith believes the committee provided a good opportunity for communication. "It kept the door open for talking. Even if we didn't always get our way, the door was still open." Whether all the right people participated during this process is debatable. Two New Mexico gaming tribes—the Pueblo of Pojoaque and the Mescalero Apache Tribe—have refused to accept the new compacts. The fact that all the gaming tribes did not participate made it difficult for some legislators to agree to anything, because they did not want to repeat the process with other tribes. Senator Carlos Cisneros recognized the process would be easier with full tribal representation and participation. The absence of the two tribes may have illustrated to legislators that each tribe is a distinct government entity and, with regard to certain issues, each may have to be addressed separately. That the Pueblo of Pojoaque and the Mescalero Apache Tribe were invited to be part of the process certainly speaks to its openness.

A number of the parties involved felt that the process, in general, was successful. John Yaeger, assistant director for the Legislative Council Service and staff for the Committee on Compacts, recognized that " ... the process brings a degree of order to what otherwise could be a confusing three-way negotiation." In addition, although the committee considered the proposed compact during the 2000 legislative session but did not approve it until the 2001 session, Richard Hughes said the process "went exactly as it was supposed to." He also noted that the process was not simply a repeat of the tribal negotiations with the governor's office. "The committee picked up on different issues than the governor's office did. It came out a much better product than it would have otherwise." Senator Smith agrees: "The process worked pretty smooth. You knew where everyone was coming from. It was a very methodical method for working through the issues."

Although the face-to-face negotiations with the governor were likely a more effective forum for the tribes to raise their issues, in dealing with the Committee on Compacts, it was more difficult for tribes to put forth new issues because they were primarily responding to legislative concerns. Also, although committee members seemed willing to hear from everyone, their patience and time were limited because they were asked to hear a good deal of testimony. Hughes would make no real changes in the process, however. "It gave the Legislature ample opportunity to have their views incorporated." More importantly, he added, it accomplished a crucial goal. "It ensured that what was ultimately voted on was what the (11) tribes had basically agreed to."

Section 2. State Commissions and Offices

Approximately 34 states have an office or commission dedicated to Indian affairs. These offices and commissions generally are established to serve as a liaison between the state and tribes, and are concerned with interests specific to American Indians and tribes. Although these offices and commissions vary in their structures and specific roles, typical duties include reviewing and facilitating tribal comments on proposed legislation and other state policies; assessing the needs of the state's American Indian population; facilitating cooperative projects and programs between the state or local governments and the tribes; and serving as a clearinghouse for information about tribal-state issues. These commissions generally do not have significant decision-making authority but, instead, act as a vehicle for tribal input into state processes. Like the legislative committees, these commissions also can be subject-specific, such as Montana's State-Tribal Economic Development Commission. That group was formed under a 1999 bill to work on improving economic conditions on the state's seven reservations, with the belief that improved reservation economies will help the state as a whole.

Many of these offices are called "Governor's Office of Indian Affairs." Several were created after World War II, when the federal government was pursuing a policy of terminating relationships with Indian tribes and states were beginning to play a greater role in law enforcement and relocation efforts on reservations. The "Governor's Office" model can be effective if the governor is committed and the office is well-staffed with people who are willing to reach out to the tribes and to the state legislature and the state agencies. Over time, however, these offices have become inconsistent in their effectiveness. New governors may not have the same commitment to the office, which limits the outreach abilities of the staff. Such offices also have often been targeted for budget cuts. The ensuing isolation within the governor's office limits the ability of the office to play an effective facilitation or liaison role.

Most commissions are established through legislation. Commission members generally are appointed by governors and tribes; in some instances, legislative members are appointed by legislative leadership. Membership often is a mix of Indian and non-Indian members, although in most, Indian members constitute a majority. Non-Indian members typically include legislators, governor and attorney general representatives, and representatives of various state agencies. Commission leadership is elected or statutorily appointed. Commission staff usually includes, at the very least, an executive director and, because these bodies are state entities, commission or office staff are state employees. In Idaho, however, the state and tribes share staffing responsibilities. Commission and office operation usually are funded through the state's general fund, although publication sales and federal grants also may add to their budgets.

As in the case of legislative committees, commission effectiveness varies, based on several factors. Some suggestions follow for successful commissions.

- Ensure that members are representative of their communities, are committed to the process, and have some measure of independence from the governing bodies of the state or tribes (governor, legislative leadership, and tribal leadership).

- Commit adequate staff who are well-suited to the broad range of issues and the high demand for outreach, facilitation, networking and information sharing.

- Establish bipartisan commission leadership or alternate between parties.

- Ensure that commission procedures are conducive to full participation by all members.

- Base creation and operation of the commission on mutual needs and mutual commitment of the state and tribes.

In a session at the 2000 NCSL Annual Meeting, Barbara Warner, executive director of the Oklahoma Indian Affairs Commission, offered this advice.

> You need to have an Indian affairs office that is viable and is funded if you want to have available that kind of assistance to work out some of the problems you have ... Tribal issues are so broad it's just unfathomable at times. You

need to have someone who can understand all those things, and how different things affect tribes and the state. You need to have someone who can really communicate, not only with your legislature, your executive branch and your tribes, but who also can help facilitate that communication so that everybody is reading from the same page in the same hymnal ...

Sometimes our legislators don't understand that, although state legislation cannot directly affect the tribes, it can inadvertently do so and create problems in the long run. We're there to take a look at the legislation and figure out how it would affect the tribes, if at all, and communicate that to the tribes so they, in turn, can do their own lobbying.

Minnesota Indian Affairs Council

Minnesota Governor Luther Youngdahl expressed the need to improve communications with and services to the American Indian community at a Governors' National Conference held in Minnesota in 1949. He proposed that states establish Indian affairs commissions to meet that need. Minnesota was the first state in the nation to establish an Indian affairs agency. The Minnesota Indian Affairs Council (MIAC), established in 1963 (MN Statutes Chapter 888, §2 (3:922)), is the official liaison between the state of Minnesota and the 11 tribal governments within the state. The MIAC executive board is composed of the 11 tribal chairs or executive officials, two at-large members (who live in Minnesota and run for election), three senators and three representatives (appointed by the respective majority parties), and the governor's nine cabinet members. The MIAC plays a central role in the development of state legislation and administers four programs designed to enhance economic opportunities and protect cultural resources for the state's American Indian constituencies. It also monitors programs that affect the state's American Indian population and tribal governments. Unemployment, education, housing and health issues are a few of the issues addressed by the council.

In addition to working directly with the 11 tribal governments, MIAC provides a forum for and advises state government on issues of concern to urban Indian communities. The Urban Indian Advisory Council (UIAC), appointed by the MIAC board of directors, is an active subcommittee of the Indian Affairs Council. The purpose of the UIAC is to advise the MIAC board on the unique problems and concerns of Minnesota Indians who reside in urban areas within the state. UIAC members include five Indians enrolled in Minnesota-based tribes, with at least one who resides in each of the following cities: Minneapolis, St. Paul and Duluth. The UIAC meets every other month in various urban areas.

Governor Jesse Ventura has held three meetings with tribal governments to date during his term in office. He spent an entire day on the Fond du Lac reservation visiting preschool children, touring community development sites and meeting with tribal elders. Establishing a good working relationship with the governor has been paramount for the MIAC. In 2001, the MIAC hosted a tribal summit for county commissioners that featured a presentation entitled *Everything you wanted to know about Indians but were afraid to ask*. A panel of tribal leaders and attorneys were present to answer questions about treaties, tribal governments, and state and tribal relations. After four hours of frank discussion, county and tribal participants in the summit, realizing their common interests, spontaneously decided to visit the state Legislature together.

According to MIAC Executive Director Joe Day: "Minnesota and tribal governments have institutionalized many programs specifically to meet the needs of Indian tribes. We have compacts and agreements that meet the needs of both parties. That's not to say that there's no room for improvement—there is. The challenge for us is protecting the sovereignty of tribes. The education and re-education of mainstream America is a never-ending task on the local, county, state and federal levels. We've been around for quite a while and accomplished a lot. We have cross-deputization between tribal and county law enforcement, low-interest housing loan programs, and scholarships for post-secondary education since 1955. We provide a forum for states and tribes to get together and get tribes more involved in policymaking. We've been doing it for

15 or 20 years. The challenge is not to slip into complacency. We need to rethink our strategies now. We're working with the state Legislature on establishing a Native American caucus. Next, we need to strengthen relationships between the state Legislature and Indians who have moved off the reservation. We need to provide better delivery of services to them and to do more outreach." (For more information about the Minnesota Indian Affairs Council, see http://www.indians.state.mn.us/.)

Oklahoma Indian Affairs Commission

Oklahoma is home to 38 federally recognized tribes, representing a population of more than 500,000 American Indian citizens. The Oklahoma Indian Affairs Commission was created in May 1967 during the 31st session of the Oklahoma Legislature. The commission's mission is set by statute to serve as the liaison between the Indian people of the state, Indian leaders of the state, tribal governments, private sector entities, the various federal and state agencies, and the executive and legislative branches of the Oklahoma state government.

The commission is made up of 20 members; nine are tribal members appointed by the governor with the consent of the Senate, and 11 are non-voting, ex-officio members. A 15-member advisory committee comprised of individuals with expertise not otherwise represented by the commission board play an important role in short- and long-term planning. Four of the appointed members are from tribes represented by the Bureau of Indian Affairs' Muskogee Area Office, four are from tribes represented by the Bureau of Indian Affairs' Anadarko Area Office, and one member serves at-large. The 11 non-voting, ex-officio members represent various state elected officials and state agencies.

The four primary goals of the Oklahoma Indian Affairs Commission are to:

- Develop state and federal legislation;
- Maintain an advisory committee;
- Develop and implement research projects and reports; and

- Develop cooperative programs between tribes and state, federal, local and private entities; health organizations; educational agencies; and economic development and tourism entities.

The commission pursues these goals through activities such as legislative development and tracking, written reports and publications, sponsorship of various forums, and regular meetings with tribal leaders. In addition, the Oklahoma Indian Affairs Commission responds to inquiries from the general public and serves as an information conduit between the tribal governments and local, state, and federal governments and agencies.

"One of our primary jobs is to encourage government-to-government relationships," says Commission Executive Director Barbara Warner. "That type of relationship lies within the executive branches of both state and tribal governments, and it is at this level that we maintain that any issues can be addressed and ultimately resolved. Using this top-level approach rather than a bottom-up approach has resulted in more expedient results while maintaining the government-to-government relationship process."

"We're viewed as the single point of contact between the state and tribes," Warner comments, "We are also considered somewhat of an authority on state and tribal issues and are often called upon to present testimony or provide insight from the tribal perspective, which is information that we gather directly from tribal leaders. A lot of what we do involves educating the state and public about American Indian issues, tribal government, and culture, a task that is never-ending." On the other hand, the commission also helps tribes to navigate state policymaking processes by keeping them informed of legislative activities. Warner feels that high levels of communication and accurate, factual information are some of the keys to the commission's success. "We take our role very seriously when it comes to providing as much accurate and factual information as possible in order to bridge the gaps of misunderstanding that may exist for Indian and non-Indian audiences alike—and people can count on that," Warner concludes. (For more information on the Oklahoma Indian Affairs Commission, see http://www.state.ok.us/~oiac/.)

Oregon Legislative Commission on Indian Services

In 1975, the Oregon Legislative Commission on Indian Services (CIS) was statutorily created to improve services to Indians in Oregon. Its 13 members are appointed to two-year terms jointly by the Senate president and the speaker of the House. CIS consists of one member from the Oregon Senate, one member from the Oregon House of Representatives, representatives from each of the nine federally recognized tribes, and two representatives from the urban Indian population in Oregon. CIS members select their own officers to serve one-year terms.

Under its enabling statute (ORS 172.100), CIS has the following responsibilities: 1) to compile information about services for Indians; 2) to develop programs to inform Indians about services available to them; 3) to advise public and private agencies about the needs and concerns of the Indian community; 4) to assess programs of state agencies operating for the benefit of Indians and recommend program improvement; and 5) to report biennially to the governor and the Legislative Assembly on all matters of concern to Indians in Oregon.

CIS has broad statutory responsibilities concerning the protection of cultural resources in Oregon. In addition, CIS provides consultation services to state agencies when its administrative rules require them to discharge duties relating to American Indians or cultural resources. These may include, for example, the Children's Services Division in Indian child welfare matters, the Water Resources Department in hydroelectric development activities or the state historic preservation agency in cultural resource issues.

CIS recommends methods for the state of Oregon to improve its services to Indians and to improve its relationship with tribes in Oregon and in Indian communities. CIS holds regular meetings to learn about the issues that concern Indian people and to discuss how these issues might best be addressed. CIS monitors legislation that may affect Indians, both while it is being considered by the legislature and after it becomes law. CIS also notifies people about legislation in which they are interested and assists in coordinating and presenting testimony on issues of importance to Indians in Oregon. CIS serves as a resource and advisory body to the executive branch, the legislature and state agencies and also functions as an information clearinghouse about state government and Oregon's Indian communities.

"Prior to the establishment of CIS, there was no mechanism in state government to consider Indian concerns directly," says Karen Quigley, CIS executive director. "CIS serves as the main forum in which Indian concerns are considered. It serves as a conduit through which concerns are channeled to the appropriate entity; it serves as a point of access for finding out about state government programs and Indian communities; and it serves as a catalyst for bringing about change where change is needed."

Section 3, on government-to-government agreements and protocols, contains a discussion of the agreement and the "cluster group" system that the CIS has developed to implement the state-tribal relationship in Oregon. For more information about CIS, see http://www.leg.state.or.us/cis/cisset.htm.

Section 3. State-Tribal Government-to-Government Agreements and Protocols

The establishment of guiding principles for a government-to-government relationship between state executive branches and tribes has been a significant development in recent years in state-tribal relations. The 1989 Washington *Centennial Accord*, discussed below, outlines a state-tribal relationship that " ... respects the sovereign status of the parties, enhances and improves communications between them, and facilitates the resolution of issues." Most recently in Oregon, the state legislature codified the state's government-to-government policy, which directs state agencies to develop tribal consultation policies to include tribes in the development and implementation of state programs that affect tribes.

Written policies also are found in states such as Alaska, Michigan and New Mexico, although they vary in some respects in form and in content. The agreements provide mutual commitments of states and tribes, whereas executive orders address only the state's role. What such policies and agreements have in common is respect for tribal government and a commitment to consult and coordinate on state actions that may significantly affect an Indian tribe or its members. Although these policies serve as a significant—and even historic—policy commitment, they are also intended to be only guiding principles, not legally enforceable commitments.

The state-tribal policies trace their origins to the long-established relationships between Indian tribes and the federal government. The terminology of a "government-to-government" relationship that is based on a consultation process originated in the 1970s as part of the Tribal Self-Determination Policy initiated by President Nixon. This federal-tribal relationship is embodied in a series of federal policy documents begun by President Reagan in 1984 and expressed most recently in Executive Order 13175, signed by President Clinton on November 6, 2000, entitled "Consultation and Coordination with Indian Tribal Governments."

Centennial Accord between the Federally Recognized Indian Tribes in Washington State and the State of Washington

The Centennial Accord in Washington was signed in 1989 by Governor Booth Gardner and by the leaders of 26 of the state's 27 tribes. The accord was conceived as the result of a controversial debate over treaty fishing rights in the 1970s and 1980s. The disagreements over treaty fishing were public and contentious and at times affected issues that were unrelated to fishing, such as health care and child services. According to Mel Tonasket, who was chairman of the Confederated Tribes of the Colville Reservation at the time, "We needed to find a way to work together and establish that we could disagree on some issues, and still find ways to cooperate on other issues. The bad blood between the state and the tribes was causing too many good opportunities to be lost for both sides. The Centennial Accord was an effort to establish cooperation where we had common interests."

The Centennial Accord primarily focuses on establishing respect for the governing authorities of both the tribes and the state, without attempting to define exactly what those authorities are. It also focuses on the mutual responsibilities that both the state and the tribes have for making the relationship work. The accord establishes an annual meeting between the governor and the tribal leaders. Finally, the Centennial Accord has a strong focus on providing information to those in state government about Indian tribes and their status as independent governments. The accord does not specifically address relationships between the tribes and the state legislature; those parties have recently been considering several proposals for the development of a legislative committee that would address tribal issues.

In practice, the document serves as an important historical touchstone for an improvement in the tribal-state relationship after the treaty fishing "wars." Primarily, the document serves the need to establish respect for tribal governments. According to Chairman W. Ron Allen of the Jamestown S'Klallam Tribe, "Prior to the Centennial Accord, anytime we went into a state agency or office, tribal leaders almost always had to explain the very basics of who we were, the federal treaties, and why we had a right to be involved in that particular issue. It was like we were always starting from zero, so it was very difficult to resolve anything. The Centennial Accord helped to fix that, so that the state people at least began to understand who we are and why our government-to-government relationship is important."

In addition to the training component of the Centennial Accord (discussed in section 9), an annual meeting between the governor and the tribes has been established. This annual meeting, which has taken place every year since 1989, is seen as a positive step in building communications between the tribes and the governor. However, it is clear that the annual meeting alone is not enough. At a tribal-state summit meeting in November 1999, the following statement was fairly typical of those voiced by a number of tribal leaders; "We meet every year with the governor and complain about the things that are wrong, then we go away and nothing happens until the next year. We need some follow-through and regular communication throughout the year to make sure that change is implemented."

The 1999 meeting resulted in a commitment to better institutionalize the Centennial Accord. This agreement, entitled *Institutionalizing the Government-to-Government Relationship in Preparation for the New Millennium*, focuses on concrete actions to build channels of communication, institutionalize government-to-government processes that will promote resolution of issues, and implement a consultation process.

The Centennial Accord is generally regarded as a successful policy that is respected by both state and tribal officials. The Governor's Office of Indian Affairs is an excellent source of information about the accord; a copy is also available on the Internet at www.goia.wa.gov.

Oregon Statute and Executive Order on Tribal-State Relations

In a first-of-its-kind development, the Oregon legislature, in 2001, passed a bill (S.B. 770) addressing the state-tribal relationship in Oregon. The law requires state agencies to promote communication and government-to-government relations between the state executive branch and the tribes. Specifically, the law requires state agencies to develop policies to:

- Identify programs that affect tribes and the state employees who are responsible for those programs;

- Establish a method to notify state employees about the policy; and

- Promote "positive government-to-government relations" and communications between the agencies and tribes.

Other provisions of the law include:

- Encouragement to use agreements between states and tribes, authorized under a separate statute (ORS 190.110.);

- Direction to the Oregon Department of Administrative Services to provide annual tribal issues training to state agency managers and employees who have regular communication with tribes;

- Direction to the governor to convene a meeting once a year where the state agencies and the tribes can work together to achieve mutual goals; and

- Requirements that state agencies are to submit an annual report on their activities under the statute.

The statute does not create any right of action or a right of review of an agency action.

Although the Oregon law is new, it is based on Executive Order 96-30, which was signed by Governor Kitzhaber in 1996. In turn, the drafters in Oregon cite the Executive Memorandum on Government-to-Government Relations signed by President Clinton in 1994 as the template for the Oregon executive order. The executive order contains the same four basic elements as the new law: an annual summit of tribal and state agency leaders, training for key state employees, designation of key contacts, and a general requirement for intergovernmental cooperation to work together on mutually agreeable goals and solutions.

The Oregon statute and executive order are part of a successful approach to state-tribal relations that has developed in Oregon. Like the Centennial Accord in Washington, the Oregon policies build respect for and knowledge about tribal governments and urge cooperation. The Oregon policies go further in that they direct each state agency to develop its own specific policy on state-tribal relations and to report annually to the governor and the commission.

The Oregon Legislative Commission on Indian Services, discussed in section 2, serves a key role in implementing the statute and the executive order. "Obviously, a document like an EO is a guide giving direction—you have to check out the implementation," says Karen Quigley, the executive director of the commission. The commission, with a strong focus on follow-through, serves as a liaison, facilitating group and information clearinghouse.

The most innovative tool for implementation of these policies is the "clusters groups" that have been developed by the tribes and the state of Oregon. The cluster groups are state/tribal workgroups that are set up in six broad topic areas:

- Natural Resources,
- Cultural Resources,
- Public Safety and Regulation,
- Economic and Community Development,
- Health and Human Services, and
- Education.

These groups meet three or four times per year, and combined tribal and state participation has been 20 to 30 people per meeting. There is a deliberate effort to encourage consistent representation by state key contacts and tribal counterparts. The experience in Oregon has been that regular meetings in the cluster groups have been successful in creating the permanent, ongoing communication and relationships that are necessary to address issues in the early stages of policymaking and move away from the reactive, crisis-to-crisis mode of intergovernmental relations that has been predominant in state-tribal relations.

Karen Quigley describes the key features of the cluster groups in her paper, *Oregon's Three-Point Approach to State/Tribal Relations*:

> Some "clusters" meet for one-day sessions, some for two days. Most clusters alternate sites—a reservation one meeting, a state agency hosts the next. Each cluster usually devotes a portion of the time to a description of Tribal programs and State agency programs, including structures

and "culture" of both Tribes and State agencies. All clusters work to maintain an updated contact list and all clusters try to acknowledge the importance of the "social" aspect of the relationship-building and so include as part of the program, a shared meal, shared entertainment or a field trip, e.g. to a shell midden or a tour through a series of state agency buildings to get a chance to actually see the contrast among state agencies and compare their respective resources. Some clusters have focused on creating legislative proposals, some on developing state-wide management plans, e.g., in the area of cultural resources protection, some have focused on "matching up" state programs with specific Tribal needs, like investment or development possibilities.

Significantly, the clusters provide a rich opportunity for state agencies to hear about each other's programs and resources (we often forget that state agencies don't necessarily act in a coordinated fashion—they often don't even know that much about each other). In addition, the cluster meetings offer another rich opportunity that was not necessarily part of the original design: tribal department heads and staff get to interact with and hear from their counterparts in other Tribes. Without a doubt, there has been an impressive amount of information-sharing and working on joint solutions that has occurred in the clusters.

Alaska Millennium Agreement

The governor of Alaska and 63 tribal leaders signed the *Millennium Agreement between the Federal Recognized Sovereign Tribes of Alaska and the State of Alaska* in April 2001. This agreement creates a framework for government-to-government relations between tribal governments and the state and builds upon a governor's administrative order that recognized the sovereignty of Alaska's tribes. To date, approximately 80 of Alaska's 227 tribes have signed the agreement.

Tribal government leaders from Alaska began a discussion with Governor Tony Knowles in 1999 about the possibility of creating a government-to-government relationship between the State of Alaska and the Alaska Tribes. According to Mike Williams, the chairman of the Alaska Inter-Tribal Council, the intent was to improve the communications and the atmosphere, so that the tribes and the state could begin to work on the problem areas. "Our state and our Native communities have very real problems that must be addressed, and the state needs the tribal governments at the table in order to tackle these issues. There is a great need for coordination to address issues such as the decline of subsistence fisheries and the need for economic development, and basic services such as education, health care, substance abuse treatment and law enforcement. The tribal governments and the state have common interests in addressing these issues, but we needed a way to set up a more constructive dialogue before we could start."

Governor Knowles responded at the December 1999 Annual Meeting of the Alaska Inter-Tribal Council (AITC) by offering to begin a process of negotiations to create a written agreement for government-to-government relations in Alaska. Tribal leadership in Alaska considered this offer at a meeting in Anchorage in February 2000 and agreed to form a negotiating team of 46 tribal leaders to represent the various tribes from different regions of the state. This group, which met with state administration officials numerous times throughout 2001, was co-chaired by Joe Williams, president of the Saxman IRA and vice-chair of AITC, and Bruce Botelho, the Alaska attorney general.

The first—and very significant—achievement of the negotiating team was Administrative Order 186, which was signed by Governor Knowles on Sept. 29, 2000. That order directed state agencies and officials to "recognize and respect" the 227 federally recognized tribes in Alaska. The order was the first step in the governor's efforts toward a more cooperative relationship between Alaska's tribal governments and the state. The order also rescinded a 1991 executive order signed by former Governor Hickel that denied the existence of tribal governments in Alaska. After this order was signed, the negotiating team turned its energy toward the Millennium Agreement.

The Millennium Agreement sets out the assumption of mutual respect between the state the tribes and also sets a framework for future communications. One of the most promising aspects is the agreement to set up working groups or committees that will meet regularly to discuss specific issues in greater depth. This mechanism offers the opportunity to build long-term relationships and networking between state and tribal officials that will help to address issues. However, the agreement does not address any substantive issues; those are to be addressed in the future through the communications processes set up under the agreement.

According to Will Mayo, the governor's senior advisor on rural and tribal policy, the implementation of the Millennium Agreement has posed challenges and offered some early rewards. The governor's office began immediately to work with the commissioner of each state department to develop the key contacts and the internal polices for each of the departments; most of these have been completed and signed. The working groups also have been meeting to work on some of the longstanding problems, and these meetings have significantly augmented the communications. They now are beginning staff training on tribal issues. "These have been the most positive things," says Mayo. "We are building new pathways for communication between the tribes and the state that have never existed before." Joe Williams agrees: "The state agencies are beginning to work with us, and this is a very positive change."

One goal of the agreement was to develop a permanent institutional structure for the state-tribal relationship. The structure committee was formed and made a recommendation for a permanent office within the state administration. However, funding for this office has not been provided by the Legislature, and the state and tribes continue to work on this issue. The challenge will be to implement the communications mechanisms in the Millennium Agreement and sustain them over a long period of time, particularly through the next change in administration.

Another significant challenge has been gaining participation by the tribes in the policy building process. There are 227 federally recognized tribes in Alaska, and the large number of tribes, in addition to their remoteness and diversity, make communications a very big job. Adequate participation at routine meetings is difficult to arrange, and most of Alaska's tribes have very few resources to contribute.

Finally, the Millennium Agreement serves as a strong foundation with the governor's office, but it does not address the relationship with the state Legislature. More work will be necessary to begin the communications process between the tribes and the state Legislature. The Alaska Inter-Tribal Council plans to step up its efforts to meet with legislators and hopes to build the same kind of focus found in the Millennium Agreement: meeting the needs of native and non-native citizens, building communications and finding possible areas of cooperation in lieu of jurisdictional battles.

Section 4. Tribal Delegates in State Legislatures

Maine

Maine currently is the only state with tribal delegates to the state legislature. In fact, there have been tribal delegates in the Maine Legislature since 1820, although American Indians in Maine did not have the right to vote in state elections until 1967. In Maine, the two delegates are provided for in legislative rules. Penobscot Representative Donna Loring and Passamaquoddy Tribal Delegate Representative Donald Soctomah are granted seats on the floor of the House. The delegates are elected by their tribes, are entitled to per diem and expenses for each day's attendance during session (3 MRSA §2), and are not subject to term limits as are other Maine representatives. They participate in committee processes and floor debate, but they have no vote in committee or on the House floor. Tribal delegates can introduce legislation on tribal issues and co-sponsor any legislation. The Legislature recently amended House rules to allow the delegates to offer floor amendments to the legislation they introduce.

The presence of the delegates in the House provides a general education to other legislators. "It absolutely helps other legislators become educated on Indian issues. They admit that themselves," Representative Donna Loring recognizes. "Even when we're losing (on a particular bill), we're still up there on the policy level educating legislators and everybody else." As Representative Judy Kany stated in 1975, the delegates " ... give this House the benefit of the Indian's first-hand knowledge and at the same time allow them at least a voice in the state's policymaking process which affects their lives."

> **Maine House Rule 525**
> Penobscot and Passamaquoddy Tribe. The member of the Penobscot Nation and the member of the Passamaquoddy Tribe elected to represent their people at the biennial session of the Legislature must be granted seats on the floor of the House of Representatives; be granted, by consent of the Speaker, the privilege of speaking on pending legislation; must be appointed to sit with joint standing committees as nonvoting members during the committees' deliberations; and be granted such other rights and privileges as may from time to time be voted on by the House of Representatives.
>
> **Maine Legislature's Joint Rule 206(3)**
> Indian Representatives. The member of the Penobscot Nation and the member of the Passamaquoddy Tribe elected to represent their people at each biennial Legislature may sponsor legislation specifically relating to Indians and Indian land claims, may offer floor amendments to this legislation, may cosponsor any other legislation; and may sponsor and cosponsor expressions of legislative sentiment in the same manner as other members of the House.

In addition to dramatically improving communication between state legislators and tribal leaders, the delegates lend a new and unique perspective to the political debate in the Legislature. The system also provides an avenue for tribal members to learn about the state Legislature. The Maine delegates send a newsletter to their tribes that contains information about the legislative process and bills they are sponsoring and co-sponsoring.

The delegate model also lends itself to early tribal involvement in legislative processes, since tribes are not waiting for legislators, staff or their lobbyists to inform them of legislative proposals, but are present when legislative measures are proposed and debated. Although the two delegates cannot be in every committee hearing on bills of interest, they generally are made aware of relevant bills through an informal network.

The lack of a vote for the delegates has been discussed in the past few years. The state attorney general has opined that allowing the delegates to vote would be unconstitutional and would violate the "one person, one vote" principle, which the U.S. Supreme Court has defined as " ... the vote of any citizen is approximately equal in weight to that of any other citizen in the State." (*Reynolds vs. Sims*, 377 U.S. 533, 579 (1963)). Representative Loring laments, "If you can't vote, you're tied—you don't have the cards to play like the others, but you just still need to work to convince people. It's like if you lose one of your senses, you compensate with another."

Representative Loring hopes to address the issue of voting in committee soon. Other issues that proponents would like discussed include potential tribal representation in the Maine Senate and representation of the Micmac (that apparently have not been interested in representation in the past) and Maliseet tribes in the Legislature. Chief Brenda Commander of the Houlton Band of Maliseets has indicated it would be helpful to have a delegate from her government in the Legislature.

Wisconsin

State legislators and tribal leaders in Wisconsin have debated allowing tribal delegates in the state Legislature. Senate Majority Leader Chuck Chvala, speaking in favor of the proposal, noted that, "Speaking on the floor is a very powerful role ... Native Americans will be in a unique position to influence policy and public opinion." In addition to how many tribal delegates there should be (since Wisconsin has 11 tribes), the issue of whether the delegates would vote has been debated. Some observers are concerned that giving tribal delegates a vote could pose constitutional challenges of double representation because tribes already are part of the constituencies that other elected legislators represent (the "one person, one vote" issue). Others are concerned that the lack of voting privileges would relegate the Indian delegates to a token position where they are involved in a process in which they have no voice. Still others conclude that the positions would be what the individuals make out of it.

Many agree that, even without voting privileges, the tribal delegate model could provide meaningful representation, give tribes a voice early in the legislative process, provide fuller tribal involvement, and facilitate a deeper legislative understanding of issues that affect tribes. Some Wisconsin legislators believe it would be helpful to have tribal representatives involved in the process so tribal positions would be aired about issues that are raised. Legislation was introduced in 2001 in the Senate (S.B. 230) and in the Assembly (A.B. 478) to create tribal delegates; however, the bill did not progress.

South Dakota

South Dakota considered a bill (H.B. 1210/S.B. 68) in 2001 to create tribal delegates to the Legislature. Senator Ron Volesky, who sponsored the bill, says that, "It would do a lot to improve relations between state and tribal governments." A member of the Standing Rock Sioux tribe, Senator Volesky proposed to have nine delegates in the House, one from each tribe. The bill failed in committee by a vote of six to three.

Virginia

Virginia also considered a resolution (H.J.R. 615) to create a joint subcommittee to study whether to seat representatives of the state's eight officially recognized Indian tribes as nonvoting members of the General Assembly. Recognizing that " ... a beneficial relationship between the Commonwealth and its Indian tribes hinges on fostering cooperative assistance, consultation and sharing of information to promote mutually shared interests," the resolution was tabled in the Committee on Rules by a vote of 16 to one.

The Delegate Model

Many practical questions are raised by the delegate model: How would tribes decide to select delegates? Who would the delegates represent—their own tribe, a caucus of tribes, or all tribes in the state? Should there be qualifications a person must meet to serve as a tribal delegate? Should tribes have some sort of intertribal forum to advise the delegates? In addition to these questions is the concern about access to legislative staff and a budget, which are considered critical to the success of the delegate model. Finally, all legislatures have numerous committees. What would be a tribal delegate's role in committee and in which committees could the delegates participate? These questions raise fundamental—including constitutional—issues. They would require careful consideration by any state and tribe interested in this option.

Section 5. Intertribal Organizations

Intertribal organizations are membership organizations that may represent all or some of the tribes in a state or a wider region. Although intertribal organizations are not a substitute for intergovernmental relationships with individual tribes, they can perform many useful functions, such as assisting in the dissemination of information to tribal governments. State legislators may wish to address the tribal leaders in their state at an intertribal organization meeting where tribal leaders may be gathered to discuss common interests. Depending on resources and staff, intertribal organizations may perform a variety of other functions, including tracking legislative activities and facilitating tribal input into legislative processes.

Regional and issue-focused intertribal organizations also may exist within a particular state. The Midwest Alliance of Sovereign Tribes and the Montana/Wyoming Tribal Leaders Council are examples of regional intertribal organizations that represent the interests of member tribes. The California Indian Manpower Consortium, the Northwest Portland Area Indian Health Board, and the Northwest Indian Fisheries Commission are state or regional issue-focused intertribal organizations. (A listing of many state and regional intertribal organizations can be found in *Government to Government: Understanding State and Tribal Governments.*)

Great Lakes Intertribal Council

The Great Lakes Intertribal Council (GLITC) is a consortium of federally recognized Indian tribes in Wisconsin and Upper Michigan. Started in 1963 as a community action agency, it was a vehicle for delivery of services and programs to its member reservations and the rural Indian communities of Wisconsin. With the increase of local tribal government authority and capacity, the member tribes have assumed more responsibility for administration of services to their own communities. Consequently, the role of GLITC has changed from one of direct service provider to one of assisting the member tribes in a delivery system of services and programs to support and supplement the tribes' own service capacity.

The tribal chairman or the chair's designated representatives of each member tribe comprise the GLITC board of directors. The board conducts its business at monthly meetings held on a rotating basis at one of the 11 tribal government headquarters. Day-to-day business of the organization is conducted from the central office located in Lac du Flambeau, Wis.

Although GLITC supports the tribes' independence, it also provides a forum for tribes to discuss, resolve and address those issues that require intertribal unity and attention. Political action, intergovernmental relations and policy decisions find an intertribal discussion forum through GLITC but, by long-standing custom, public comment and policy implementation are reserved to the member tribes through their elected representatives.

State legislative staff David Lovell finds that GLITC is useful in providing a point of contact and an entry into tribal government communication. Lovell says, "GLITC is useful in helping me to make communication with tribal governments. GLITC staff have deeper personal relationships with tribes. They can identify the people at each tribe that I should be talking to." "On the other hand," Lovell notes, "intertribal organizations are a two-edged sword. The danger is that state officials may rely too heavily on intertribal organizations, substituting relationships and consultation with intertribal organizations for true government-to-government relationships with individual tribes."

Robert Chicks, chairman of the Stockbridge-Munsee Tribe, echoes Lovell's comments. "This is a government-to-government relationship between the individual tribe and the state. But GLITC plays an important role because the Wisconsin tribes have a lot of common interests as well. I think GLITC plays a big role in helping state legislators to understand the lay of the land, and they are a good source of technical information. For the tribes, our intertribal organization can help us work collectively and mobilize to participate at the critical moments, assisting tribes in responding to the state process." (For more information about the Great Lakes Inter Tribal Council, see www.glitc.org.)

Inter Tribal Council of Arizona

The Inter Tribal Council of Arizona (ITCA) was established in 1952 to provide a united voice for tribal governments located in the state of Arizona to address common issues of concerns. On July 9, 1975, the council established a private, nonprofit corporation, Inter Tribal Council of Arizona Inc. under the laws of the state of Arizona to promote Indian self-reliance through public policy development. ITCA provides an independent capacity to obtain, analyze and disseminate information that is vital to Indian community self-development. The purpose of the corporation is to provide the member tribes with the means for action on matters that affect them collectively and individually, to promote tribal sovereignty, and to strengthen tribal governments.

The members of ITCA are the highest elected tribal officials: tribal chairpersons, presidents and governors. These representatives are in the best position to have a comprehensive view of the conditions and needs of the Indian communities they represent. As a group, the tribal leaders represent governments that have a shared historical experience. Consequently, the tribes have a common governmental status in addition to similar relationships with federal and state governments.

ITCA operates more than 20 projects and employs a staff of 50 to provide ongoing technical assistance and training to tribal governments in program planning and development, research and data collection, resource development, management and evaluation. ITCA staff also organize and conduct seminars, workshops, conferences and public hearings to facilitate participation of tribal leaders in the formulation of public policy at all levels. The goal of ITCA and its commitment to the member tribes is to ensure the self-determination of Indian tribal governments through their participation in the development of the policies and programs that affect their lives.

ITCA Executive Director John Lewis has worked for many years to improve the relationship between the 21 Arizona tribes and the state of Arizona. Lewis notes, "It's challenging work. The people change, on both the state and tribal sides. We work toward pro-Indian policies with the different state agencies. Relationships with some agencies are better than with others." Regarding their relationship with the state Legislature, Lewis adds, "Our work has been not so much passing [pro-tribal] bills as stopping [anti-tribal] bills. The Legislature did, however, establish a Tribal Nations Day at the state Capitol."

Lewis believes intertribal organizations have a unique role in tribal-state relations. "Often, tribes need to have a united effort in going to the Legislature to make things happen. Agencies are subject to budgets and directives set by the Legislature. Tribes and intertribal organizations, as an outside force, can get things done. We can work with the executive branch and legislative branch on issues in a way that is mutually reinforcing." (For more information on the Inter Tribal Council of Arizona, see http://www.itcaonline.com/.)

Section 6. Dedicated Indian Events at the Legislatures

Several states—such as Arizona, Maine, New Mexico, Oklahoma and Oregon—designate specific days during their legislative sessions for interaction with tribal governments. Some of these events are institutionalized in statute. During these "Indian days," tribal leaders and members come to the capitol to engage in various activities aimed at building relationships with the legislators and

Models for Cooperation

communicating their legislative priorities. Tribal leaders may address one or both houses of the legislature. Some states, in fact, host an annual or biennial "state of the tribes" address, in which one or more tribal leaders formally address a joint session. For instance, Blackfeet Chair Earl Old Person delivered a "State of the Tribal Nations Address" to the Montana Legislature in February 2001. In his address, he discussed Indian heritage and its relationship to Montana, sovereignty, health, education, and many other issues of importance to the Indian communities.

During dedicated Indian days in the legislature, tribal leaders may meet with committees or individual legislators. Tribal governments also may set up information booths in the capitol rotunda, give speeches, or provide dancing and craft exhibitions. Tribal leaders or elders also may be given an opportunity to offer a blessing or invocation at the commencement of the senate or house sessions for one or more days.

These days may be tied to social events, such as annual dinners or receptions. Social events can effectively build relationships, so long as both tribal leaders and legislators participate. The effectiveness of these events varies. Although ceremony is important for mutual respect, cultural understanding and formality, dealing with the real issues—and having an accountable process for doing so—is crucial. Events should include some opportunity to discuss specific proposals or issues. One tribal official says that tribal leaders may not participate if they think it is all simply for show and no real legislative efforts will result. Likewise, some legislators may not participate if tribal leaders discuss only generally such issues as tribal sovereignty and offer no specific proposals or projects that legislators can actually work on during the session.

Arizona Indian Nations and Tribes Legislative Day

Indian Nations and Tribes Legislative Day was enacted to " ... pay tribute to the history and culture of the American Indian peoples and their contributions to the prosperity and cultural diversity of the United States" (Statute 41-1108). Several components characterize this event in the Legislature. The evening before the legislative day, the Indian Council of Arizona hosts a reception to which legislators and tribal leaders are invited to meet and mingle. The next morning, legislators assemble in joint session to hear tribal leaders address the Legislature, followed by a luncheon sponsored by the Indian tribes for state and tribal leaders. In the afternoon, breakout forums are held to address various issues—such as economic development, transportation, health, education and others—in which the state and tribes share a common interest in or jurisdiction.

Senator Pete Rios recalls when the event was formalized in 1994 in order to have a day of recognition and appreciation of Indians that would be more than just a social gathering. Unfortunately, the participation of the state legislators and tribal leaders has waned over the years, especially in the afternoon session when tribal and state leaders have the opportunity to voice and hear opinions on issues of mutual concern. Senator Rios is concerned about the lack of participation, which he attributes to cultural insensitivity and lack of education regarding tribal culture and ways.

Ron S. Lee, executive director of the Arizona Commission of Indian Affairs, agrees that " ... the breakout sessions do not amount to much of anything because nothing is really discussed or settled. No hard core issues or actions come out of it, including legislation." Both state and tribal leaders seem to be losing interest in the event. According to Lee, fewer state legislators attend because they feel there is no value to the breakout forums because of other priorities, and the implementation of term limits does not allow enough time to focus on every issue before them. Lee also adds that tribes are " ... not prioritizing specific items or projects. They're still talking about general ideas." The event does not appear to foster continuous dialogue between the state and tribes that might occur from contacts made at the event or issues that may be raised. It is more a day of ceremony and recognition than a time to deal with issues, produce results or work on resolutions.

Previously, this event has been planned and organized by a group independent of the Legislature. However, discussions are taking place to involve the Legislature in the 2002 session activities. The reason for more involvement according to Representative Sylvia Laughter (also chair of the Native American Affairs Committee), is that " ... the legislature is concerned with feedback that they have received about the ineffectiveness of the day." She also comments that the purpose of the event has not been accomplished and it needs to be refocused on all of the 21 tribes in the state. Some legislators wanted to do away with the event all together; however, Laughter thought that improvements could be made, including inviting urban Indian representatives. She also explains that, "The Legislature would like to implement necessary changes to be consistent with the statutes as directed." The statutes require the Legislature to observe Indian Nations and Tribes Legislative Day, to invite tribal leaders to a joint assembly, and enjoin the Legislature to " ... schedule activities and discussions between state and Indian nation and tribal leaders on major issues, particularly those for which the state and Indian nations and tribes share a common interest or jurisdiction." Laughter sees the Native American Affairs Committee's involvement as a progressive move, and she encourages legislators and interested organizations to be more involved and to work together to accomplish the intent of the law.

Oklahoma American Indian Business Day at the Capitol

The Oklahoma Indian Affairs Commission co-sponsored the first American Indian Business Day at the Capitol in March 1999 with the American Indian Chamber of Commerce; the event has continued each year since. The goal of the event is to heighten awareness of American Indian businesses in Oklahoma through exhibits and interaction among vendors and legislators. A diverse pool of about 30 American Indian and tribal businesses from across the state set up booths in the Capitol rotunda, and legislators are encouraged to visit the booths and meet with various business owners.

J.T. Petherick, deputy director of the Oklahoma Indian Affairs Commission, says the intended results of the event are to communicate the economic benefit contributed to the state by the tribes. "Through this legislative day ... we have really raised awareness of the economic impacts of tribes to legislators." Excluding tribal governments, the Indian-owned businesses contributed an estimated $2.4 billion annually and, if tribal government contributions are combined with that figure, the economic benefit to the state of Oklahoma is approximately $10 billion annually.

The event has virtually no negative aspects. It offers an opportunity for legislators and Indian businesses to interact, but its success depends upon participation. Businessman Michael Kelly, president of the Oklahoma Chapter of the American Indian Chamber of Commerce, states that, "How well you do depends on how actively you promote yourself. The more people you meet the better you do. Some businesses get more out of it than others."

In addition to the exhibits, legislators and businessmen make presentations about economic and business issues. Senator Kelly Haney addresses those gathered to welcome them to the Capitol and to recap the financial and economic contributions that the tribes make to the state. One significant contribution concerns employment. The number of people (tribal members and non-tribal members) employed by the tribes is higher than the total number of American Indians in the state.

This event provides an opportunity for legislators, tribal leaders and tribal business people to make contacts and obtain information and to show how much Indian and tribal businesses contribute to the state. Everyone agrees that more businesses should be able to attend, set up displays and make contacts. Although space in the Capitol is limited, the commission hopes to expand the event to enable more businesses to attend and perhaps to eventually include other Indian organizations.

Section 7. Individual Legislator Efforts

Individual legislators can make efforts to address tribal issues, either in their general capacity as state officials or in their responsibilities to constituents.

- Legislators can organize and sponsor issue-specific roundtable meetings or hearings with tribal leaders, as some Nebraska legislators have recently done to address the issue of tribal gaming.

- If sufficient resources are available, a legislator may hire specialized staff to advise him or her about Indian issues, as did California Senate Minority Leader Jim Brulte in 2000.

- Legislators can meet with tribal leaders in their district on a regular basis or can provide constituent services as for any other citizen, such as intervening if there are particular problems with a state agency.

- Legislators can participate in committees that are of interest to tribal constituents and in established state-tribal institutions.

- Legislators also can introduce bills that benefit tribal constituencies and ensure that tribal governments are aware of bills that may affect them.

American Indians and Alaska Natives who are elected to state legislatures, although they do not directly represent their specific tribal government, can provide representation for their unique community needs. In 2001, 46 known American Indian legislators held office in 14 states. Alaska had the largest delegation with 12, followed by Montana with six and Arizona and New Mexico each with five. Many have said that they feel they have a dual role: to serve as an official for the good of the entire state and also to attempt to protect the unique interests of their tribal communities. Similar to the Maine tribal delegates, these legislators are able to educate their colleagues, from the inside, about tribal governments and Indian issues. That often includes dispelling stereotypes, according to Arizona Representative Debra Norris, who is Navajo and Blackfeet.

Wisconsin Representative Frank Boyle

Individual legislators can provide leadership to promote communication and good relations between states and tribes. The chair of a legislative committee with appropriate jurisdiction can use that position to address difficult issues and to foster improved relations. One example comes from the Wisconsin Legislature's Special Committee on State-Tribal Relations (formerly the American Indian Study Committee).

In 1990, at the height of the often violent controversy over the off-reservation spearfishing rights of the Lake Superior Chippewa Bands, Representative Frank Boyle, then the committee's chair, held a public hearing of the committee in the affected area of the state to allow Indians and non-Indians to discuss the issue and to express their feelings and frustrations. Representative Boyle prefaced the hearing by saying that he would rather that unhappy citizens hurl epithets at the committee than hurl rocks and bottles at the boat landings. The hearing lasted seven hours and included testimony from invited dignitaries, including the six Chippewa tribal chairs and the state attorney general, and more than 30 members of the public. The testimony was frank on the part of all participants, but the proceeding was more dignified than many other discussions of this topic. Representative Boyle held another hearing the following year, with similar results.

Representative Boyle followed up on these hearings by organizing a fact-finding trip to Washington in 1991. A delegation of leaders from the legislative and executive branches of state government (led by the speaker of the Assembly), and from the six Chippewa band governments met with their counterparts in Washington to hear how conflicts over the use of fish resources were resolved. The purpose of the meetings was to find ways to bring similar resolution in Wisconsin. This trip, in turn, led to the formation of a State-Tribal Natural Resource Task Force, chaired by Representative Boyle and charged to develop projects for the cooperative management of natural resources by the state and tribal governments for the mutual benefit of all citizens. The task force met for more than a year and developed nine separate project proposals.

These activities—the hearings, the fact-finding trip and the task force—did not by themselves resolve all the conflicts relating to spearfishing, but they did contribute to the resolution. In particular, they fostered communication between citizens and between governments. They gave state and tribal government officials at all levels—from resource managers working in the field to top policymakers—experience in working together to solve common problems. They also helped to forge working relations—many of which remain in place today—between those government officials. What is more, they were the result of the leadership of one legislator.

Oklahoma Senator Kelly Haney

Senator Enoch Kelly Haney (D-Seminole) has been key to the state and tribal relations in Oklahoma. As one of the relatively few American Indians who is serving as a state legislator, he has worked diligently to promote communication and cooperation between the state of Oklahoma and the tribal governments located within the state. His most notable accomplishments have come in the areas of state-tribal agreements, economic development and cultural preservation.

In 1988, Senator Haney became the first chairman of the Joint Committee on State and Tribal Relations, which was established to allow legislative approval of state and tribal agreements. Since its inception, the joint committee has played an important role in the development of agreements in gaming, cross deputization and social welfare, among others. Senator Haney also has been actively involved in other state and tribal agreements that do not require joint committee approval, such as those involving motor fuels and tobacco. More than 175 state and tribal agreements exist in Oklahoma, demonstrating the spirit of cooperation in the state.

In 1994, Senator Haney authored legislation creating the Oklahoma State-Tribal Economic Development Task Force, designed to evaluate various resources that are available for economic development, identify jurisdictional barriers that may hinder economic development efforts, recommend methods to develop joint state-tribal economic activities, and report findings and legislative recommendations to the governor. He also has actively promoted the economic contribution of tribal governments in the state through video projects, a Web site, and participation in the "American Indian Business Day at the Capitol" (see section 6).

Cultural awareness and preservation are a priority for Senator Haney. Perhaps the most significant endeavor is his work to develop a Native American cultural center in Oklahoma, scheduled to open in 2004. The facility will celebrate the diverse histories, cultures and achievements of all Native American tribes and nations. He also has worked tirelessly to promote the history and culture of American Indian tribes in Oklahoma through various art, education and historical programs. *(Prepared by J.T. Petherick, deputy director, Oklahoma Indian Affairs Commission.)*

Section 8. State Recognition of Native Cultures and Governments

States, through their legislatures, have acknowledged and honored American Indians as individuals or groups in many ways. Such recognition is frequently independent of the task of addressing particular issues. This approach allows states and tribes to put aside contentious issues to focus on building relations.

State legislatures recognize and acknowledge native cultures through the passage of a variety of bills and resolutions. Approximately 37 bills have been introduced in the states during the past four years that, among other things, have honored specific American Indian tribes; created days, weeks and/or months to acknowledge native contributions made to the states; and removed offensive terms from geographic place names. Altogether, 27 states observe days, weeks or months commemorating American Indians and, in some cases, these dates are considered state holidays where public schools and other organizations may be encouraged to commemorate American Indians through appropriate activities such as educational and cultural exhibits.

Some states also have enacted legislation that prohibits the use of the term "squaw" and requires its removal from geographic features. States have required the term to be removed from maps, signs and markers as they are updated; created a council or group to develop replacement names; or simply prohibited the use of offensive names.

State Recognition of Indian Tribes

Twelve states—Alabama, Connecticut, Delaware, Georgia, Louisiana, Maine, Massachusetts, Michigan, New Jersey, New York, North Carolina and Virginia—have officially recognized more than 40 American Indian tribes as separate and distinct governments within their borders. In several of these states, the recognition has occurred through legislative action. The main reason tribes have petitioned for state recognition is to receive acknowledgment and recognition of tribal existence and to foster a continued government-to-government relationship with the state. Greg Richardson, director of the North Carolina Commission on Indian Affairs, comments that, "State recognition is a whole new dimension in Indian affairs."

Although state-recognized tribes are eligible for substantially fewer benefits than federally recognized ones, there are some tangible benefits. State-recognized tribes receive protection under the federal Indian Arts and Crafts Act of 1990—under which tribal members may proclaim their Indian status on their art work—and under the federal Native American Free Exercise of Religion Act of 1993. State-recognized tribes also can apply for limited federal programs such as education, job training and housing assistance; however, the services of the BIA and the IHS are not available to them.

Other benefits are at the discretion of each state. Alabama, Connecticut, Louisiana and North Carolina, for instance, may allow application for programs and services; provide funds for education, entitle membership on commissions established to address American Indian affairs, and allow input on state Indian policy, issues and legislation.

Just as there are a variety of benefits for state-recognized tribes, there also are a variety of guidelines and procedures states use to determine recognition. The state's criteria may be based on those used for federal recognition, or the recognition may consist of a simple legislative proclamation. Alabama, North Carolina and Virginia have a commission or council on Indian affairs that has the authority to officially recognize tribes.

Richardson comments that, "There is a lack of understanding why the state recognition process is important and needed." Some state officials fear that recognition of a tribe will lead to the establishment of casinos within their state boundaries. For tribes to conduct gaming activities, however, they must be federally recognized, according to the Indian Gaming Regulatory Act of 1988.

Finally, merely applying for recognition does not ensure that it will be granted. It takes time to gather supporting documentation to meet the criteria and it also takes time to review the information once an application has been submitted. In some cases, applicants do not qualify and are denied recognition.

American Indian Artwork in the Statehouses

States can recognize the contributions of Native cultures and individuals through displays or permanent fixtures. In perhaps the most striking example, Oklahoma plans to place a 17-foot statue of an American Indian warrior atop its Capitol dome. Called *The Guardian*, the bronze statue is being sculpted by Seminole Indian Kelly Haney, who also is a prominent state senator. "I think it represents Oklahoma," said Senator Haney. "The story of the native people in Oklahoma is really the story of the history of Oklahoma."

There are other examples, as well. In California, the Legislature is placing a commemorative seal that honors American Indians—and that was created by an American Indian—on the front steps of the state Capitol. The Wyoming Legislature recently installed a statue of Chief Washakie in the Capitol rotunda. Although the Legislature appropriated $180,000 to help pay for the statue, it is

Models for Cooperation 59

not clear whether the statue will remain on capitol grounds or will be placed on some state property in the city. Utah has a statue of Chief Massasoit at the front steps of the Capitol building. In Wisconsin, a portrait of Chief Blackhawk, a 19th century Sac and Fox tribal leader, hangs in the Assembly parlor. Although it is not on the statehouse grounds, Nevada voted to allow a statue of Winnemucca, a Paiute activist and educator in the late 1800s, to be included in the U.S. Capitol Statuary Hall. Each state is allowed two statues in the hall.

Although such symbolic mechanisms may not directly address specific policy issues, they are important in educating, creating good will and building relationships.

Section 9. Training for Legislators and Tribal Leaders on Respective Government Processes

Both state legislators and tribal government leaders benefit from training about the structure of one another's governments and the respective decision-making processes. Not many states or tribes have instituted this important function, although a few states have produced materials, as discussed below. Tribal leaders feel that the lack of understanding about tribal governments is one of the most significant stumbling blocks to better tribal-state relations. The reverse is also true, however. State bureaucracies—including the state legislative process—can appear convoluted and confusing. It also is important that tribal leaders understand state government processes. Whether the tribes or the state provides the training for tribal leaders, and whether the state or the tribes provide the training for legislators, some institutionalized educational process is crucial to good relations.

A variety of training tools and processes can be useful for this purpose.

- General materials, such as the NCSL and NCAI publication, *Government-to-Government: Understanding State and Tribal Governments*, are helpful to provide background on the issue.

- State- and tribe-specific information also is important because states—and, especially, tribes—vary widely in government structure and process.

- Training need not be limited only to written materials. Workshops or training sessions, however brief, often are helpful to relay information.

- Training could be included in new legislator orientation and in an equivalent session for tribal leaders.

- Training could be combined with an annual social function for legislators and tribal leaders, providing a more relaxed, less formal atmosphere that also would encourage interaction between state and tribal officials.

- Finally, training also may be provided for legislative and tribal leader staffs, who often conduct research on particular issues.

State Training Materials

Two state legislative staff offices have produced handbooks on tribal issues. The Montana Legislative Council published *The Tribal Nations of Montana: A Handbook for Legislators* in 1995. This book includes sections on many major state-tribal relations issues, including Montana's Indian tribes, principles of state-tribal relations, tribal sovereignty and state power, civil and criminal jurisdiction in Indian country, economic development, Indian gaming and others. "When the Handbook was first written, every legislator was given a copy. We also distributed copies to the Montana Office of Public Instruction, school libraries—K-12 and higher education—every state agency, every state elected official, and tribal governments. Once people knew the handbook was available, we had numerous requests for copies from all sorts of folks, including many law school libraries all across the country. We've tried to get them into the hands of as many legislators as we can as new ones are elected," explains Connie Erickson, a research analyst with the Montana Legislative Services Division. Although they have printed the popular handbook three times, it is not routinely used in new legislator orientations, nor is there any formal policy to ensure all new legislators receive a copy. This needs to be done, Erickson agrees, "With term limits, we are experiencing tremendous turnover in our Legislature, so we probably should provide copies to every new legislator."

Research analysts in the Research Department of the Minnesota House of Representatives have produced *Indians, Indian Tribes, and State Government* (2d ed. 1998). Intended as a reference document for anyone who needs it, it originally was produced in the early 1990s when legislative staff " ... realized that Indian tribe-state relationships were coming up constantly," recalls Joel Michael, legislative analyst in Minnesota's House Research Department. The document is not distributed to all legislators, however, nor is it used in legislator orientations. Legislative staff do give various sections of the document, which are similar to the Montana handbook, to members of specific committees or to legislators who are interested in specific issues. The section on natural resources, for instance, might go to the Environment and Natural Resources Committee. Both Minnesota and Montana update these publications periodically to keep up with changes in Indian law, tribal capacities and state-tribal relationships.

First American Education Project

The First American Education Project (FAEP) is a non-partisan, nonprofit corporation that educates elected officials, the media and the public about the legal and historical relationship with and issues of importance to Native Americans. In 2001, FAEP conducted two legislative seminars on tribal law and policy, for state legislators and staff. The two events, in Washington and Connecticut, received positive feedback from both audiences.

The seminars comprised panels of Indian law experts from across the United States and discussed topics such as natural resources, taxation, jurisdiction, gaming and foundational history. Specific accommodations are made to tailor the seminars to the particular issues of interest in the state.

Perhaps most interesting has been the overwhelming interest of the audiences in historical issues. Whether it is because current issues involving litigation are both complex and unsettled or merely because the history books have long since been written and the history of how we got where we all are is our shared history, the audiences (and the panels) gained much from the extensive discussions on historical perspectives.

Prepared by: Russ Lehman, managing director, First American Education Project (www.first-americans.net).

Finally, as discussed in section 3, Washington's 1989 Centennial Accord directs the Governor's Office of Indian Affairs (GOIA) to provide training to state agencies and other interested groups on state-tribal relations and Indian perspectives. Training is held twice monthly in Olympia and once a month in an outlying community. The one-day training session covers a tribal historical perspective, legal issues, tribal sovereignty and tribal government. Attendees are provided with a user-friendly reference book, *State-Tribal Relations Training*, which contains sections on federal policy, culture, governments and economies. The manual was produced by the GOIA and has been revised four times since 1991. According to GOIA staff, the training increases the level of awareness among state employees about Indian tribes and the Centennial Accord and increases understanding of and sensitivity to tribal issues.

Section 10. Other Potential Legislative Mechanisms

Other potential mechanisms discussed by various state legislators and tribal leaders to improve relations between state legislatures and tribes have not yet been implemented.

For instance, staff positions could be created, with appropriate input from the tribes, in one or both legislative houses to act as tribal government advisors or liaisons. This person would establish and maintain a communications network with tribal leaders and intergovernmental relations staff regarding both upcoming legislative proposals that would potentially affect tribes and legislative schedules and hearing dates. This staff member ideally would be nonpartisan, could advise legislators and other legislative staff about how proposed legislation or ideas might affect tribes, and could arrange meetings between legislators and tribal leaders upon request. Accountability to both the state and the tribes would be important. Although the position may be created in statute or legislative rules, funding, hiring and supervision could be jointly overseen by the state and the tribes.

Indian affairs commission or office staff in many states already perform some of these functions, but these staff generally are responsible for interacting with state agencies and others as well. A dedicated position in the legislature would meet a need that currently is unmet in most—if not all—state legislatures.

Another idea is to require "tribal impact statements" in bills that affect tribes. Similar to fiscal impact statements, the tribal impact statements would require bill drafters to consider and acknowledge the potential effects—financial ramifications, jurisdictional implications, and programmatic and service delivery changes—of any new legislation on tribal governments. Impact statements may consist of one or two sentences for bills with very low direct impact or could include longer statements and explanations for high-impact bills. At the minimum, fiscal impact statements that most states prepare for many bills could include the fiscal effect a bill would have on tribal governments. Other options would be to have the drafter note the bills that require an impact statement and also to assign the state Indian affairs commission to prepare the statement. A bill on this topic, introduced in Wisconsin legislation (2001 Assembly Bill 772), did not pass.

Bill drafters would almost certainly require training to understand tribal government processes and to recognize the potential effects of state legislation on tribes. Training might consist of a manual developed by tribal representatives and others with input from bill drafters, coupled with annual training sessions. Tribal government liaisons, Indian affairs commission staff or others could be available for consultation with bill drafters.

There are other possibilities, as well. The Maine Senate Subcommittee of the Committee to Address the Recognition of the Tribal Government Representatives of Maine's Sovereign Nations in the Legislature discussed redrawing district lines to provide tribal members majority representation in a Senate and/or House district. That subcommittee also discussed establishing a formal process or a standard process under existing procedures for receiving comments from tribal representatives on pending matters.

5. Conclusion

As one project participant noted, "The devil is in the details." The reality is that states and tribes must work through the substance and the details of specific issues ranging from taxation to sacred sites protection. As tribes continue to expand self-governance, it will be up to the states and the tribes to tackle each one, and there is no way to shorten the hard work that is involved in these policy discussions. The point of this book is to present some options for creating a favorable forum in which those discussions can take place.

Any mechanism should be jointly developed and maintained, because it must be effective for both the states and the tribes. Both legislators and tribal leaders will want to encourage respective colleagues to become involved with these efforts. Individual states and tribes will need to decide what is realistic and practicable in their particular situation. Jamestown S'Klallam Chairman W. Ron Allen suggests an approach of "aggressive incrementalism" because the greatest progress often is made through small steps. However it is carried out, a commitment to cooperation and early and regular information-sharing, education and relationship building are the keys to finding common ground in addressing the needs of all constituents—both Indian and non-Indian.

APPENDIX

The appendix includes examples of state-tribal agreements in various subject areas, to show how these agreements have benefited the states and the tribes and, in some cases, to give some information about how the agreements originated. The examples themselves make an impressive case for the value of cooperative agreements and hopefully will inspire the state and tribal leaders who are working through these types of policy issues.

Law Enforcement and Cross-Deputization Agreements

Law enforcement in Indian country can be a complicated issue, but the goal is straightforward—to protect public safety and "catch the bad guys." The simplicity and urgency of this goal provides great opportunities for cooperation that are realized on a daily basis throughout the country.

There are a variety of scenarios where the federal government—Bureau of Indian Affairs (BIA)—the state, local and tribal governments or a variation of these have jurisdiction on tribal land and over tribal members. Law enforcement and cross deputization agreements between tribes; state, county and city police officers; and the BIA are becoming more abundant across the country. Because jurisdictions and boundaries often are blurred or nonexistent between tribal areas or reservations—which are often checkerboard—and local or state jurisdictions, the need for assistance from other law enforcement officers is steadily increasing. These agreements expand coverage and services to all citizens in the area; therefore, people feel safer, there are shorter response times by officers to calls for help, and more law enforcement coverage is available without added expense to state, local or tribal departments.

Because crime rates are on the rise across the country—including on and near Indian reservations—the need for additional law enforcement personnel is essential. However, budget constraints prevent hiring new officers or adding extra patrols and, therefore, citizens are increasingly more vulnerable. These agreements generally contain procedures for emergency backup, pursuit of a criminal across boundaries, and arresting and issuing citations on another agency's turf. Some areas are so large that dispatching an officer from another jurisdiction may be the quickest way to bring law enforcement to the scene of a crime.

To understand the following retrocession agreement in Montana, an explanation of the federal law, Public Law 83-280 (more commonly referred to as PL 280) is necessary because Montana is one of the states that falls under the scope of this federal law. Public Law 280—passed in 1953 during the time of termination and forced assimilation of Indians by the federal government—was subsequently amended in 1968. It effectively took away the shared jurisdiction between the federal government and tribes involving Indians in Indian country, gave the states criminal jurisdiction over Indians on reservation lands, and opened state courts to civil litigation. The law placed a financial burden on the states because it failed to provide funding for enforcement.

Six "mandatory" states—Alaska (after statehood in 1958), California, Minnesota, Nebraska, Oregon, and Wisconsin—were required to assume jurisdiction, thereby allowing the federal government to relinquish its special criminal jurisdiction involving Indian perpetrators or victims. The tribes in these states were not consulted. However, the Red Lake Band of Chippewa Indians in Minnesota, the Confederated Tribes of the Warm Springs Reservation in Oregon, and the Metalkatla Indian Community in Alaska were able to successfully demonstrate that they had satisfactory law enforcement mechanisms in place, strongly opposed being subjected to state jurisdiction and, therefore, were exempted from PL-280. Other tribes unsuccessfully tried the same approach.

To relieve the financial burden on the states for implementation and enforcement of PL 280, the 1968 Civil Rights Act gave the states that had assumed jurisdiction the option to return all or any measure of jurisdiction to the federal government and the tribes. The federal government would have final say over the retrocession and, again, Indians had no say in the matter. However, this would allow tribes the possibility—and, for some, the eventual reality—of re-obtaining jurisdiction over civil and criminal matters over Indians on their lands.

Ten "optional" states—Arizona, Florida, Idaho, Iowa, Montana, Nevada, North Dakota, South Dakota, Utah and Washington—elected to assume full or partial state jurisdiction over tribes after the 1968 amendments were in place. Some of these states consulted with the tribes within their borders and assumed jurisdiction of some with tribal consent.

Flathead Reservation—Montana Highway Patrol Retrocession Renewal

Because Montana is one of the optional PL 280 states, the decision to return jurisdiction to the Confederated Salish and Kootenai Tribes of the Flathead Reservation was requested by the tribes and, in 1994, the state Legislature agreed and retrocession became reality. The Flathead Reservation tribes were the only ones in Montana over which the state exercised PL 280 authority, and they requested retrocession concerning misdemeanors on tribal land. According to a Flathead tribal attorney, the tribe originally wanted full retrocession or to take over all law enforcement on the reservation, including felony crimes, but the state did not agree. State, county and local law enforcement agencies currently have jurisdiction over felony crimes on the reservation.

In September 1999, the Confederated Salish and Kootenai Tribes of the Flathead Reservation; the state of Montana; the counties of Missoula, Sanders and Flathead; and the local governments of

Ronan, Hot Springs and St. Ignatius signed a renewal of the original 1994 law enforcement agreement, also referred to as retrocession. Lake County and the City of Polson chose not to sign the agreement or the renewal.

Lake County commissioners, at the behest of law enforcement personnel, declined to sign the agreement because they were led to believe that it would return tribal jurisdiction over misdemeanor crimes to the tribes and would not become a cross-deputization agreement, although that is what ultimately occurred. Missoula County signed the agreement, and Commissioner Barbara Evans explained that the decision about and input for the agreement were left to local law enforcement personnel because they would be affected and would have to work with the tribe. Lake County commissioners felt that the county's liability risks were too high and that, under the agreement, the county would not be protected should someone decide to sue a tribal officer. Polson Mayor Mike Lies also was concerned about the lack of prosecution of tribal members arrested by city officers. Although they did not sign the agreement, the local and tribal law enforcement officers have a working relationship, according to Lake County Commissioner David Stipe. Flathead Chief of Police Ron McCray agrees that law enforcement personnel work well together and relations are good, but that everything would be easier if the two had signed the agreement.

The original retrocession agreement authorized the return of jurisdiction over misdemeanor crimes committed by Indians to the tribes on the Flathead Reservation. It authorized law enforcement personnel (state highway patrol and local and tribal officers) to stop any vehicle for a traffic violation and enforce laws involving minors in possession of alcohol. Before retrocession, these offenses had been prosecuted in state court since the early 1960s under Public Law 280. However, the state retains its jurisdiction over felony offenses committed on the reservation.

This reciprocal agreement allows either tribal or nontribal officers to respond to calls when dispatchers call the nearest officer to respond or for officers to stop vehicles for suspicion of criminal activity, whether or not the suspect appears to be Indian. A suspect, if claiming Indian descent, must present proof that he or she is an enrolled member of a federally recognized tribe. The agreement requires the responding officer to detain the suspect and call the appropriate authorities once the suspect is identified as Indian. If the appropriate law enforcement officer is unable to respond to the scene, the responding officer—with the consent or granted authority of the appropriate authority or officer—may issue a citation or, upon arrest, transport the individual to the appropriate facility for processing.

All parties involved in the agreement are required to meet once a year throughout the term of the agreement to discuss implementation issues, changes in law or processes that affect the agreement, or other concerns. State and tribal prosecutors were required to meet bimonthly for the first six months and thereafter to review the frequency of meetings needed. These meetings allow the open exchange of information on pending cases and ensure that each jurisdiction is, in good faith, prosecuting the cases appropriately.

Tribes will continue to retain concurrent jurisdiction with the state over felony crimes committed by Indians, but they may transfer prosecution of such crimes to the state and the state may transfer prosecution to the tribes if warranted. The retrocession agreement continues until 2002, when it will be up for renewal.

Environmental Agreements

Indian tribes have been given increasing authority by Congress to administer environmental programs under federal environmental protection statutes. Tribes benefit from environmental regulatory authority—they can set their own priorities concerning the balance between development and natural resource protection and can find the most culturally appropriate ways to manage resources and protect the environment. These recently (relative to state programs) developed tribal environmental programs, however, often cause concern for state regulators as well as for pollution sources. For example, tribes can set air or water quality standards that vary significantly from state standards, which can cause difficulty for either government to effectively implement their programs, and also can cause difficulty for regulated sources to comply. Air and streams flow freely between one jurisdiction and another. That is also the reason that environmental and natural resources management provide good opportunities for collaboration—pollution and natural resources respect no political boundaries. These are shared resources that all governments have a stake in protecting. As such, some states and tribes have decided to work together to accomplish these goals rather than add to the rich history of environmental litigation over such issues.

Air Quality Control Agreement Between the Southern Ute Indian Tribe and Colorado

Under the federal Clean Air Act, Indian tribes can operate their own air quality control programs within "exterior boundaries" of the reservation. The Southern Ute Tribe's 680,000 acre reservation, located in southwest Colorado, is "checkerboarded"—private land holdings dot the area within the exterior boundaries of the reservation. Natural gas and oil production is a primary air pollution source. The tribe applied in July 1998 for authorization to administer the air quality control program on the reservation, including the non-Indian owned land within the exterior boundaries of the reservation. The state of Colorado objected on that issue. In fact, the tribe and state had been arguing over air quality authority on the reservation for more than 10 years. They may have been headed to court, but the state and tribe decided to discuss, not litigate, according to John Cyran with the Colorado Attorney General's Office, who helped negotiate the agreement.

An agreement was finalized to establish a single collaborative authority—the six-member Southern Ute Indian Tribe/State of Colorado Environmental Commission—to promulgate rules and regulations for the reservation air quality program. The commission of three members appointed by the governor and three appointed by the tribal council will be the policymaking and administrative review authority.

Appendix

Once approved and in place, the day-to-day administration and enforcement will be administered by the tribe. Colorado Governor Bill Owens signed the agreement for the state, but it needed legislative approval. The Colorado legislature provided the framework and authorization for the state to enter the agreement. The Southern Ute Tribal Council also approved the agreement. The tribe will include the air quality standards set by the commission as part of its application to the U.S. Environmental Protection Agency for delegated authority to administer an air quality program. The parties currently are waiting for congressional approval of the agreement.

The parties still do not agree about who has regulatory jurisdiction over these lands, but this is not relevant in light of the agreement they reached. The real issue to be resolved, said Cyran, was how best to regulate air quality in a checkerboarded area. Nothing in the agreement affects state or tribal sovereignty or constitutes a waiver of state or tribal immunity for any purpose.

As the parties recognize in the text of the agreement, "[t]he State and Tribe, as governments that share contiguous physical boundaries, recognize that is in the interest of the environment and all the residents of the Reservation and the State of Colorado to work together to ensure consistent and comprehensive air quality regulation on the Reservation without the threat of expensive and lengthy jurisdictional litigation."

The parties agree on a multitude of benefits expected to result from the agreement:

- Duplicative efforts and monetary and program resource expenditures by the state and the tribe will be minimized.

- Certainty is created for regulated sources on the reservation about who is the regulator.

- The program will be developed in such a way that it reflects particular interests of the tribe, yet is compatible with state air quality goals.

- State technical assistance will be provided to the tribe.

Finally, both parties concur that the agreement " ... eliminates the risk of a protracted and costly jurisdictional dispute, which dispute would potentially include the tribe, state, EPA and regulated parties."

Tax Agreements

The administration of state and tribal taxes on tribal lands has caused a great deal of misunderstanding over the years, but it also has proven to be a fertile ground for states and tribes to reach compacts and agreements. Nearly every state that has Indian lands within its borders has reached some type of tax agreement with the tribes. According to a report issued by the Arizona Legislative Council, in 1995 more than 200 tribes in 18 states had created successful state-tribal compacts that were mutually satisfactory to both parties. Many more agreements subsequently have been reached. As tax laws, and economic conditions inevitably change in the future, this is an area that will require continuing attention by both state and tribal governments.

Tribal governments have the authority to collect taxes on transactions that occur on tribal lands, and tribal government revenues are not taxable by state governments. In addition, states cannot tax tribal citizens who live on and derive their income from tribal lands, but those who work or live outside tribal lands generally are subject to state income, sales and other taxes. Like state and local governments, tribal governments use their revenues to provide services for their citizens. Unlike state governments, tribal governments most often are not in a position to levy property or income taxes. Income from natural resources, tribal businesses, and sales and excise taxes are most often the only non-federal revenue source.

The more complex rule regarding state taxation sales between Indian sellers and non-Indian buyers is the source of most of the misunderstandings in this area. The Supreme Court has held that state governments can collect excise taxes on sales of imported products to non-members that occur on tribal lands, so long as the tax does not fall directly on the tribal government. In practice, this rule creates difficulties in administration because it depends upon the identity of the purchaser, rather than on the jurisdiction where the transaction takes place. Tribal governments also disagree with this ruling because it results in the inequity of dual taxation, where tribes are prevented from collecting their own sales taxes because of the resulting double tax burden, and the tax revenue flows off-reservation.

States and tribes have developed a variety of methods for addressing these issues, often through intergovernmental agreements or through state statute. Some states have chosen to recognize tribal sovereignty and have exempted such sales from state taxes altogether. Others have entered into agreements for the collection and distribution of taxes, which can take the form of intergovernmental compacts or state statutes.

Most recently, the Winnebago Tribe of Nebraska and state officials ended a gas tax dispute with a precedent-setting agreement. "This is the first opportunity when I saw a representative of the state actually come to the tribe and want to help," said Shawn Bordeaux, vice chairman of Ho-Chunk Inc., the Winnebago tribe's business corporation. Janet Lake, the state's motor fuels division administrator, explained that " ... one of the things Governor Johanns has always supported is that we have a government-to-government relationship" with tribes. The compact specifies that the tribe and state agree to a revenue-sharing process, with the tribe collecting 75 percent of taxes from reservation-based gas sales. It then sends a quarterly check to the state for the state's 25 percent share.

Some states and tribes have entered into agreements that simply exempt Indian purchasers on reservations from paying cigarette, motor fuel or other sales taxes. Utah has an agreement with the Ute Tribe exempting all cigarette sales to tribal members from state taxes. Wyoming has the same type of agreement with the tribes in that state. Wisconsin exempts from taxation all motor fuel sales to Indians on reservations.

Other states have accomplished the same result by reaching agreement with tribes for an allocation of the product to be taxed (usually tax-free cigarettes) to on-reservation retailers, set by a per capita consumption formula reflecting the number of Indians (or tribal members) residing on the reservation. Under these agreements, tax-free cigarettes can be sold to Indians or tribal members, and state taxes must be collected on sales to non-Indians.

Several states have entered into agreements with tribes under which the tribe adopts the same tax as the state. In some cases, a revenue split is agreed upon wherein the tribe takes the tax revenues attributable to on-reservation sales to Indians, and the state takes the revenues attributable to sales to non-Indians. In other cases, states have agreed that tribes may keep all the tax revenues from the "single tax," whether the on-reservation sales are to Indians or non-Indians. This system treats on- and off-reservation sales to non-Indians equally, eliminating double taxation by the state and tribes that would create a disadvantage for economic activity on reservations. Unlike the tax sharing approach, this type of agreement allows tribes to retain all tax revenues from on-reservation sales, whether to Indians or non-Indians, just as the state retains revenues from off-reservation sales, regardless of whether the consumer is Indian or non-Indian.

With growing frequency, states are turning to pre-collection of taxes at the wholesale level, before the product ever reaches retailers. In the case of motor fuels, for example, a majority of states have shifted to taxing at the "terminal rack"—the point where barges and shiploads of motor fuels are transferred into truck-size tankers. About 1,300 such terminal racks exist in the United States. Of the 33 states that have federally recognized tribes, at least 27 states have enacted terminal rack or first sale from distributor collection laws. These new laws often have necessitated renegotiation of tribal-state tax compacts.

A number of states have exempted all on-reservation sales from state taxation. These states avoid double taxation of a transaction by both a tribe and a state and recognize such sales as an important source of income for tribes. This approach acknowledges to the fullest extent possible the need for any government to make its own taxation decisions in order to fund governmental services and/or to encourage economic development.

Several examples follow of the many effective tax agreements currently in place between state and tribal governments that seek to balance tribal sovereignty and the need for a tribal tax base against the state's legal right to tax sales to non-Indians.

Nevada

In Nevada, all state sales and excise taxes are waived for the purchase of any product sold on an Indian reservation, provided that a tribal tax that is equal to or greater than the comparable state tax is applied. This applies to all sales made on Indian reservations (from cigarettes to toilet paper to a loaf of bread), with the exception of gasoline. This arrangement ensures that the 17 tribes in Nevada will have an adequate tax base and recognizes that the services the tribes provide on their reservations will benefit not only tribal members but all who enter the reservation.

Motor Fuels
In the case of gasoline sales, the state imposes a wholesale motor fuels tax on all fuel sold, distributed or used in Nevada. Although there are no motor fuels tax agreements with the tribes, tribal governments can register with the state for a refund of taxes on gasoline sold to tribal members.

Widespread support exists in Nevada for the equivalent tax agreement. Proponents include the Nevada governor, the state attorney general and retail associations. The Retail Association of Nevada has written letters of opposition to proposed federal legislation on state taxation of sales on reservations. The association views such legislation as unnecessary and counter-productive to the good relationship enjoyed between the state, tribes and off-reservation retailers in the state.

Tobacco

State officials indicate that all the tribes in Nevada that sell cigarettes or other tobacco products impose their own tribal tax and have filed cigarette tax ordinances with the state. The tribes then receive cigarettes with special stamps, indicating that the cigarettes are for on-reservation sales.

Washington

New laws passed in Washington incorporate 16 specifically identified tribes with which the Governor is authorized to negotiate cigarette-only sales tax agreements. Eleven tribes in Washington already have entered into sales tax agreements with the state. Like Nevada, Washington encourages the collection of a tribal government tax in lieu of a state tax. For the first year the measure is in effect, the tribal tax must be no less than 80 percent of the state taxes and by the third year the tribal tax must be equal to or greater than the state tax. This applies only to cigarettes. The Washington arrangement is supported by tribes, the governor and the retail industry in the state.

Oklahoma

In recognition of the sovereignty of each Oklahoma tribe, Oklahoma has reached individual agreements on a government-to-government basis with tribes in the state.

Motor Fuels

Oklahoma applies a rack tax to all fuel sales in the state. It has set aside 4.5 percent of the total taxes collected in the state as the tribal share. In order to gain access to their share of these funds, tribes sign compacts individually with the state. Each tribe receives $25,000 from the tribal share reserved by the state, and tribes that operate gas stations receive a rebate based on the number of gallons sold. The remainder of the reserved tribal share is divided among the tribes based on each tribe's resident population in Oklahoma. Disparate points of view exist in the state on this arrangement, and 10 tribes have not signed compacts with the state.

Appendix

Tobacco

For purposes of tobacco sales in the state of Oklahoma, tribes with compacts (23 as of this writing) can sell to any party, tribal member or not, and agree to remit a flat share of their proceeds to the state in lieu of taxes. The agreements make clear that there is no admission of a right for the state to tax the tribe's sales.

Foster Care Programs

State-tribal cooperation on foster care is vital for the thousands of American Indian and Alaska Native children who are over-represented in state and tribal child welfare systems. Of the approximate 405,000 Indian children that live on or near reservations, about 6,500 will be placed in substitute care every year. Although Indian tribes prefer to retain custody of Indian children and care for these tribal members in tribal child welfare systems and programs, this goal often is difficult to attain due to the lack of direct funding to tribes for foster care, maintenance payments to foster families, administrative support for state foster care programs, and training money for state worker and foster payments.

Although the U.S. House of Representatives estimates that between 3,900 and 4,600 of these children meet the eligibility standards for foster care and adoption assistance under Title IV-E, tribes are not authorized to receive Title IV-E funds directly. Especially because the average estimated monthly number of children participating in Title IV-E foster care almost tripled between 1983 and 1996—from 97,370 in 1983 to 266,977 in 1996—Title IV-E is an important funding source for the foster care and adoption of American children. One way that states and tribes have worked cooperatively on this issue, which affects Indian Country's most vulnerable citizens, is to develop state-tribal agreements that allow states to pass federal foster care funding through state governments to tribes.

Nationwide, 13 states and 71 Indian tribes have negotiated Title VI-E foster care agreements. Although no standard Title IV-E agreement exists, in general these agreements increase the ability of states and tribes to provide culturally appropriate services and allow tribes to exercise their sovereignty by implementing their own programs. A major weakness of the majority of state-tribal Title IV-E agreements is that administrative support and training money is rarely accessed by tribes. In general, most agreements are very limited, providing only for foster care payments to foster families. States and tribes that are working on Title IV-E funding agreements will want to consider the importance of allowing tribes access to administrative support and training funds for program staff and foster families.

Recently, three of the largest tribes in Washington signed agreements with the state Department of Social and Health Services, Children's Administration, empowering each tribe to operate foster care programs funded under Title IV-E of the Social Security Act. "Such agreements are significant because Title IV-E is an important entitlement funding stream for foster care and adoption services to which tribes do not yet have access," says Mary McNevins of the National Indian Child Welfare Association.

The Washington agreement has both strengths and weaknesses. Strengths include paid training costs for short-term and long-term training of personnel and full funding for staff employed by the tribe who work exclusively in foster care allowable activities. Normally, training costs are reimbursable only to state agency workers. An area for improvement in the agreement is Section 7 B, Insurance. The tribe is responsible for certifying that it can self-insure or obtain commercial insurance that may be too expensive for the tribe. It is important for states to bear in mind the limited financial resources that many tribes have. Requiring a tribe to possess costly insurance can impede a tribe's ability to receive Title IV-E funding.

Cultural Resources Agreements

Several types of cultural resources agreements exist between Indian tribes and states. Most of these agreements focus on the discovery—often during construction of buildings, bridges and roads—of human remains or burials on ancestral lands and sites that are attributed to American Indians. A series of federal laws—

the National Historic Preservation Act of 1966, as amended; the Archaeological Resource Protection Act of 1979; and the Native American Graves Protection and Repatriation Act of 1990—require contact and consultation with Indian tribes in the event of such a discovery and before intentional excavation or removal of remains and/or cultural items. State agencies that are responsible for construction projects are required to comply with federal laws when any federal money is involved with the projects.

The National Historic Preservation Act also allows federally recognized Indian tribes to assume any or all of the functions of a state historic preservation office with respect to tribal land. The decision to participate and create a tribal historic preservation office is up to the individual tribes. In addition, federal agencies are required to consult with Indian tribes that attach religious or cultural significance to historic properties, regardless of their location on or off tribal land.

Narragansett Indian Tribal Historic Preservation Office—Rhode Island Department of Transportation Monitoring Agreement

In October 1998, a unique 10-year memorandum of understanding was signed between the Rhode Island Department of Transportation (RIDOT) and the Narragansett Indian Tribal Historic Preservation Office (NITHPO). The agreement provides for RIDOT to hire tribal members as site monitors for federally funded construction projects throughout the state. Although RIDOT is still required to notify the tribe of finds of human remains and cultural artifacts, it also is paying tribal members for monitoring excavations of these burial and historic sites.

Specifically, the monitoring agreement provides for NITHPO to observe archaeological fieldwork conducted by professional archaeologists contracted by RIDOT at sites that are of Narragansett Indian significance, and for the monitors to submit their observations or comments to RIDOT on each project. RIDOT must send the archaeologists' scope of work to the tribe, which must respond with its own scope of work; both entities must agree on the cost and level of effort of the monitors. These monitors include a tribal historic preservation officer, a projects director, a tribal ethno historian and a typist. The NITHPO must submit monthly progress reports and supporting documentation as well as a record of hours worked for each employee. RIDOT agrees to compensate personal wages, mileage and overhead fees for each project. Monitors will observe the archaeological activities and conduct their own research with respect to the site. Ed Syzmanski, chief transportation projects engineer at RIDOT, says that, by working together under this agreement, RIDOT and the tribe have opened lines of communication and, even though they do not agree on everything, they are able to discuss the issues and the level of trust between them has increased a great deal since the signing of the agreement.

In both 2000 and 2001, RIDOT signed two-year agreements with the Mashantucket Pequot Indian Tribe of Connecticut (in 2000) and the Wampanoag Tribe of Gay Head (Aquinnah) of Massachusetts (in 2001) that are similar to the Narragansett agreement. However, according to Syzmanski, these agreements are much simpler and make working with the tribes much easier. These agreements provide a set payment for consultation and do not require the tribe to submit a scope of work; therefore, tribal involvement in the projects is at their own discretion. The payments are not broken down on a project-by-project basis, but are paid in installments for a set total amount for the extent of the agreement. Syzmanski states that there is a much greater level of effort and time required for each project with the Narragansett agreement, and RIDOT would rather replace that agreement with one like the Wampanoag and Mashantucket Pequot.

Once remains or cultural artifacts are discovered, they go to the state for investigation. Verification of human versus animal remains and the cultural affiliation of artifacts must be assessed prior to any return of such to the tribes. Once determination has been made, if the artifacts or remains can be attributed to particular tribes, they are contacted in compliance with federal laws and the remains and/or artifacts may be returned to the tribe.

Appendix
Mutual Respect and Equal Status Agreements

Throughout the years, state legislatures have worked with Indian tribes on a variety of issues and have passed legislation requiring and defining the states' involvement and the extent of cooperative agreements between states and tribes. Recently, more local city and county governments have realized this need and the benefits of working with nearby Indian tribes as issues of mutual concern and jurisdictions continue to arise and overlap. A result of this realization is acknowledgment of Indian tribes as separate and equal governments within state and local boundaries, and the proclamation of such with spirit of cooperation and mutual respect agreements. In addition, these agreements respect the status of a tribal government as a government equal to the city, county or state. At the local level, the governments realize the need to work with tribal governments just as they work and coordinate with any adjacent county and city governments. These agreements recognize the need for and acknowledgment of trust and status at the local community level.

Tulalip Indian Tribes (Snohomish County)—City of Seattle (King County) Government to Government Agreement

Four years in the making, this government-to-government agreement was signed in July 2000 by Seattle Mayor Paul Schell and Tulalip Chairman Stan Jones Sr. to " ... better achieve mutual goals through an improved relationship between sovereign tribal government and local city government." Each party agreed to respect the sovereignty of the tribes and the decision-making authority of the city and share respect for the values and culture of the tribes. Of the several existing state-tribal agreements, this may be the first agreement of its kind in the nation where a local or city government and a tribal government agree to respect the other's governmental status.

The agreement provides for the formation of an Intergovernmental Committee, including up to three elected officials of the tribe (the sitting chairman, the intergovernmental relations director and another elected tribal member) and the city (mayor or deputy mayor, Office of Intergovernmental Affairs director and president of the Seattle City Council), respectively, to discuss and resolve issues and to draft specific agreements to address or resolve issues of mutual concern. The full committee, which has met once since its inception, is required to meet only once a year unless issues arise that demand additional meetings. According to John McCoy, intergovernmental relations executive director for the Tulalip Tribe, the first meeting went well. McCoy also introduced a new sewer technology for the City of Seattle to consider using in their future sewer plant projects. The tribe currently is constructing the system on its reservation and has received follow-up calls from the city for information about the technology and productivity of this type of plant.

The protocol agreement lays out the framework to deal with disputes that may arise between the tribe and the city on any issue from environmental protection, cultural events, fisheries and habitat restoration. This agreement is designed to avoid future disputes by opening a continuous and permanent dialogue between the two governments rather than settling an existing problem (as most agreements are developed or designed to do). Since the tribe and the city do not share physical boundaries, the agreement does not involve jurisdictional issues. It originally came about as a natural resource issue when Seattle was constructing a water treatment plant on the Tote River. The city came across Indian artifacts and contacted the tribe because they were and are inhabitants in the area.

John McCoy and his counterpart in the Office of Intergovernmental Affairs in the Mayor's Office, David Conrad, have met several times to discuss various issues; both describe having a good relationship with each other. McCoy states that the agreement improved everything and that, within the mayor's office sensitivity to the tribe has been raised and staff now call the tribe on issues and events that they previously had not. For example, the city will call to make the Tulalip aware of construction of water or sewer lines in case Indian artifacts or remains are uncovered. The city also invites

Appendix

tribal officials, singers and drummers to present cultural segments at functions for foreign dignitaries and other visiting officials.

The Tulalip Tribe hopes that the agreement will be helpful in dealings with other cities with which they share boundaries. Some cities, according to McCoy, do not view the tribe as a legitimate government and will not work with the tribe. Conrad believes that the agreement can be used by the City of Seattle to work with other tribes in the area and that it has set a precedent that shows the city is willing and able to work with other tribes. He states that the agreement has been successful " … because it sets a tone, provides a mechanism to talk and makes sure the two governments talk." It provides structure for dialogue rather than litigation or the need for mediation and enables them to discuss the issues before they ever reach that level. Conrad also explains that it provides education regarding tribal rights and relations and advances in government and management.

There is a preliminary draft of a city Indian policy between all city departments that work with tribes and there also is a network between the Indian liaisons of the Port of Seattle, King County and the Mayor's Office. They meet at least once a month, which allows the three entities to be consistent in their relations with the tribes and policy and offers a similar idea of how to proceed with their tribal relations. Currently, and as a result of the protocol agreement, the tribe and the city are discussing a voluntary agreement on salmon productivity—to increase the number of salmon in the area—and will continue to discuss other issues as they arise.

REFERENCES

Alaska Commission on Rural Governance and Empowerment. *Final Report to the Governor*. Juneau: Commission on Rural Governance and Empowerment, June 1999.

American Indian Law Center. *Tribal-State Intergovernmental Agreements: Analysis of State Enabling Legislation* (2nd ed.). Albuquerque: AILC, 1991.

American Indian Law Center *Tribal-State Intergovernmental Agreements: Analysis of State Enabling Legislation* (1st ed.). Albuquerque: AILC 1986.

Brown, Eddie, et al. *Tribal/State Title IV-E Intergovernmental Agreements*. Portland: National Indian Child Welfare Association, December 2000.

Clark, Sue Campbell. *A Study on State Indian Commissions*. Phoenix: Arizona Joint Legislative Budget Committee, 1988.

Commission on State-Tribal Relations. *Block Grants and the State-Tribal Relationship* (draft report). Albuquerque: American Indian Law Center, 1983.

Commission on State-Tribal Relations. *State-Tribal Agreements: A Comprehensive Study*. Denver: National Conference of State Legislatures, 1981.

Commission on State-Tribal Relations. *Handbook on State-Tribal Relations.* Albuquerque: American Indian Law Center, 1980.

Cross, T.A.; D. Simmons; and K.A. Earle. "Child abuse and neglect in Indian Country: Policy issues." *Families in Society: the Journal of Contemporary Human Services* 81, no. 1, (2000): 49-58.

Erickson, Connie. *Indian Affairs Commissions in Other States.* Helena: Montana Legislative Services Division (for the Law, Justice and Indian Affairs Interim Committee), 1999.

Getches, David H. "Negotiated Sovereignty: Intergovernmental Agreements with American Indian Tribes as Models for Expanding Self-Government." *Review of Constitutional Studies* no. 1 (1993): 121.

Gover, Kevin, and James B. Cooney. "Cooperation between Tribes and States in Protecting the Environment." *Natural Resources & Environment* 10, no. 3 (1996): 78.

Johnson, Susan. *Native American Issues: 1998 State Legislation.* Denver: National Conference of State Legislatures, January 1999.

Johnson, Susan, et al. *Government to Government: Understanding State and Tribal Governments.* Denver: National Conference of State Legislatures and National Congress of American Indians, June 2000.

Kaufmann, L. Jeanne. *Native American Issues: 1999 State Legislation.* Denver: National Conference of State Legislatures, March 2000.

———. *Native American Issues: 2000 State Legislation.* Denver: National Conference of State Legislatures, December 2000.

———. *Native American Issues: 2001 State Legislation.* Denver: National Conference of State Legislatures, 2002.

———. "State Recognition of American Indian Tribes." *Legisbrief* (National Conference of State Legislatures) 9, no. 1 (January 2001).

Minnesota House Research. *Indians, Indian Tribes and State Government.* St. Paul: Minnesota House Research, 1998.

National Congress of American Indians. *A Compilation of Papers on Tribal-State Partnerships: Models of Cooperation in Government.* Washington D.C.: NCAI, June 2000.

Native American Rights Fund. *State Tribal Taxation and Summary Documents.* Boulder: NARF, 1998.

Oklahoma Indian Affairs Commission. *Oklahoma Indian Nations Information Handbook.* Oklahoma City: OIAC, 2000.

Pommersheim, Frank. *Braid of Feathers: American Indian Law and Contemporary Tribal Life.* Berkeley: University of California Press, 1995.

Quigley, Karen. *Oregon's Three-Point Approach to State/Tribal Relations.* In National Congress of American Indians. *A Compilation of Papers on Tribal-State Partnerships: Models of Cooperation in Government.* Washington D.C.: NCAI, 2000.

U.S. House of Representatives. *1998 Green Book: Background material and data on programs within the jurisdiction of the Committee on Ways and Means.* Online at http://aspe.os.dhhs.gov/98gb/11cps.htm, 1998.

Wilson, Sara, and Paula Quenemoe. *Government to Government Relations—Indian Tribes and the States.* Salt Lake City: Utah's Governor's Office and the University of Utah, 1991.